P9-AOK-771

ANNIE OAKLEY AND THE WORLD OF HER TIME

CLIFFORD LINDSEY ALDERMAN

ANNIE OAKLEY

AND THE WORLD OF HER TIME

MACMILLAN PUBLISHING CO., INC.
New York

COLLIER MACMILLAN PUBLISHERS
London

Macmillan Publishing Co., Inc.
866 Third Avenue, New York, N.Y. 10022
Collier Macmillan Canada, Ltd.
Printed in the United States of America

10 9 8 7 6 5 4 3 2 1

LIBRARY OF CONGRESS CATALOGING IN PUBLICATION DATA
Alderman, Clifford Lindsey.
Annie Oakley and the world of her time.
Bibliography: p. 85.   Includes index.
SUMMARY: Examines the life and times of sharpshooter Annie Oakley
with emphasis on her role as entertainer in Buffalo Bill's
Wild West Show and other shows of the time.
1. Oakley, Annie, 1860-1926—Juvenile literature.
2. Shooters (Farms)—United States—Biography—Juvenile literature.
[1. Oakley, Annie, 1860-1926.   2. Entertainers.
3. United States—Social life and customs—1865-1918]   I. Title.
GV1157.03A64   799.3'092'4   [B]   [92]   78-31838   ISBN 0-02-700270-5

*To the memory of Annie Oakley,
with the affection that she inspired
as I wrote this book.*

CONTENTS

ACKNOWLEDGMENTS

Acknowledgment for assistance and useful
information in the writing of this book
is made to John Hurdle, Curator, Ringling Museum
of the Circus, Sarasota, Florida; Joseph
J. Litvany, Glen Ridge, New Jersey; Betsy Lindau,
Director, Travel Council, Southern Pines,
North Carolina; Cliff Mathews, Chartwell Travel,
St. Petersburg, Florida; and Mildred B.
McIntosh, Archivist, Tufts Archives Wing, Given
Memorial Library, Pinehurst, North Carolina.

ANNIE OAKLEY AND THE WORLD OF HER TIME

BEGINNINGS

Phoebe Ann Moses, a small eleven-year-old girl, sat alone in her family's cabin, deep in thought. She *had* to find a way to improve the family's dreadful financial situation. Suddenly her attention was drawn to her father's rifle, which rested on pegs on the farmhouse wall. Curious, she decided to have a closer look. The gun was heavy, and its barrel was longer than she was tall. She had to stand on a chair to wrestle it down.

Taking a dust rag, she polished the steel-blue barrel and wooden stock. While she was working on it she slid back the bolt, opening the chamber and exposing a bullet and powder cap. The gun was loaded. As she looked out the window into the yard, a squirrel scampered across the grass and leaped to a fence rail. Its cheeks bulged until it removed a nut from its mouth and began nibbling. Dragging the rifle outside, she laboriously hoisted it to her shoulder. She had never shot a gun before, but she had seen how others went about it. Squinting down the barrel, she aimed at the squirrel's bright little eye and fired. The gun's recoil nearly knocked her over, but her aim was true; the squirrel fell to the ground, shot through the head.

This amazing feat marked the beginning of a spectacular career for Phoebe Ann, who years later would be famous throughout the world as the foremost woman sharpshooter, "Little Sure-Shot," Annie Oakley.

Annie was born on August 13, 1860, in a rude log cabin in western Ohio. The house stood on a farm in the settlement of Woodland in Darke County, close to the Indiana border and about a hundred miles north of Cincinnati. The fifth child of Susan and Jacob Moses, she was christened Phoebe Ann.

The Moses family's home had only one room. The floor was of hard-packed clay. Cooking was done over the fire in the huge fireplace, which also served to heat the cabin in cold weather. What furniture the family had was homemade. Instead of mattresses the beds had ticks of homespun cloth filled with straw. With Annie, her parents and her four sisters, Lyda, Mary Jane, Elizabeth and Sarah Ellen, all crowded into the one small room, there wasn't an extra inch of space. Jacob had to build on another room when a boy, John, was born in 1862. Two years later another daughter, Hulda, was born.

Jacob Moses was a poor man. He and his wife had moved to Darke County after their tavern in Pennsylvania was destroyed by fire. All they had was their new farm and it alone simply couldn't produce enough income to support their large family. Even when Jacob managed to get a job carrying the mail, the family continued to struggle.

Late in the fall of 1865, when Phoebe Ann was five years old, her father set out from the farm with a load of wheat and corn to be ground at the gristmill some miles away. By the time he left home the sky was a leaden gray, and it looked and felt like snow. When Jacob Moses reached the mill he left his sacks of grain to be ground and went to a general store nearby. There he bought provisions for the cold, snowbound months ahead.

By the time he started for home it had begun to snow and the wind was blowing hard. Before he had gone far he was caught in a blizzard. He barely managed to get through the blinding snow, deep drifts and bitter cold to the little log cabin. There, his wife and the older girls carried him inside. He fell ill and lay for weeks with a high fever. Often as he was delirious, he talked as if he were a young man again in his old home in Pennsylvania. He never recovered from this illness and died in the spring of 1866.

Shortly after his death Mrs. Moses married Daniel Brumbaugh, but he died soon after their daughter, Emily, was born. Now the family's situation became desperate indeed. The older children did whatever they could to help their mother. Hickory, butternut, black-walnut and hazelnut trees and bushes abounded near the cabin, and in the fall the children were able to gather a large harvest of nuts. In summer they picked wild strawberries, raspberries and blackberries that grew in the meadows. They caught crayfish in the creek and picked up apples—"windfalls"—that had blown from fruit trees. From the garden they lugged in pumpkins, which had been an important food source for settlers ever since the first colonists came to America.

It wasn't enough. Without any income, Mrs. Brumbaugh's struggle to keep her family clothed and fed seemed hopeless. Then, providentially, she was offered a job as a district nurse.

Her salary would be only a dollar twenty-five cents a week, but that was enough in those days to feed her family.

However, the job would require her to be away from home often, usually attending farmers' wives who were having babies. The older Moses girls could take care of themselves, but John and Hulda and little Emily Brumbaugh were too young to be left alone. This difficulty was solved by their neighbors, the Bartholomews, who offered to take care of the three youngest children when their mother had to be away.

Around the same time, nine-year-old Phoebe Ann (who so disliked her first name that she insisted on being called Annie) was also offered work. Mrs. Crawford Eddington, wife of the superintendent of the county home, needed help with the inmates. The inmates at the home, or "poorhouse," were people who could not make a living for themselves. Often they were old and ill. In exchange for her help, Annie would be sent to school. Although the county home was forty miles away, Annie accepted the offer. The little Woodland settlement wasn't large enough to support a school of its own, and Annie was eager to get an education.

Just how much schooling she got while she was there is not clear. It was summer when she first arrived, and school was not in sesssion. In the fall she attended some classes. One thing she did learn was how to sew well, for she helped Mrs. Eddington make clothes for the inmates.

Annie received kind treatment from Mrs. Eddington, but she wasn't happy at the institution. Some of the inmates had children who took delight in tormenting her. They even invented a singsong rhyme with which they plagued her by chanting the words "Moses-Poses" over and over. So when another job was offered she eagerly accepted it. A farmer and his wife, Mr. and Mrs. Wolf, wanted Annie to live with them and take care of their baby. She was to be paid fifty cents a week and would be able to go to school. The new job was much worse than the old one. Mr. and Mrs. Wolf were brutal people who beat her, gave her little to eat and practically made a slave of her.

Annie's work wasn't just taking care of the baby. Her life with the Wolf family was one of constant drudgery. She was up at four every morning. She prepared a substantial breakfast for the farmer and his wife, ham or bacon, fried potatoes, sometimes cornmeal mush, and coffee. Dinner, at noon, was the day's largest meal, and this too Annie prepared, as well as supper. Annie was given only leftovers. After she served her employers breakfast, she would hurry to the barn to milk the two cows. She then carried the milk to the farmhouse kitchen, strained it and brought it to the springhouse, a wooden structure over a spring in which the milk was kept cool until needed. Annie also had to feed the calves and pigs. And of course the Wolf baby required Annie's almost constant care.

She was seldom able to attend school. Although she was eleven she still could not read or write properly, so she couldn't send letters home. But Mrs. Wolf wrote to Annie's mother saying she was very happy there and was attending school regularly. When letters from home arrived for Annie, Mrs. Wolf intercepted and destroyed them.

Each day, by nightfall, Annie was so exhausted that she would fall asleep as soon as she lay down on her uncomfortable old trundle bed. One evening Mrs. Wolf found Annie nodding over a pair of stockings she was mending. The cruel woman shook her awake and beat her.

This could not go on. Annie tried hard to please the Wolfs,

but she couldn't stand the treatment she was receiving. Finally she ran away. She headed for the nearby town where she could get a train that would take her within a few miles of home. When she reached the railroad station she didn't have enough money for a ticket. Luckily, she had a friend there, a girl she had met at the school she attended while she worked for Mrs. Eddington. Her friend's mother gave Annie enough money for her fare and packed her a lunch to eat during the forty-mile trip.

Annie had been away less than two years, but she was surprised to find so much had changed at home. Her mother was married again to a farmer named Joseph Shaw, and the family was now living on his farm. All of her older sisters had married and moved away.

Annie was not impressed or encouraged by what she learned of Mr. Shaw. He was a good man, but did not seem to have a strong character. He had sold a farm he owned, intending to buy another, but had been swindled out of all but five hundred dollars of the money. With this, he was able to make a down payment on a new place, but was forced to put a large mortgage on it and the interest, which had to be paid regularly, threatened to ruin him.

Annie Moses was tired of being poor and of working at jobs that didn't improve things for her. She was not lazy, but it was frustrating that there didn't seem to be any way she could really advance herself. She did find one way to help her family live a little better. All sorts of game roamed the woods that were still all about the farm. Annie learned to snare rabbits, quail and grouse in homemade traps. They added delicious fare to the family table. But meat for dinner wasn't enough, and Annie realized that her family's lives would never really improve unless they could find a way to pay off the mortgage on the farm. It wouldn't be easy, but Annie was determined to try.

2

ANNIE'S TALENT
IS DEVELOPED

It was about this time that Annie made her first, remarkably successful shooting attempt with her father's old gun. Her mother was shocked at first and lectured her severely, but Annie wasn't to be stopped. With the rifle she could bag far more game than her rude traps could snare. Against her mother's objections she began roaming the woods and meadows toting the heavy rifle.

Now the family larder was always stocked with meat. Annie's sure aim at the squirrel wasn't just luck; the rabbits and game birds that she brought home proved that. There were far more of them than were needed for food. And that gave her an idea. One day she took a bundle of skins from some of the muskrats, beaver, minks and raccoons she had shot and a string of a dozen or so grouse and quail, dressed for the oven, and set out on foot for Greenville, fifteen miles to the south.

Annie didn't have to trudge far over the dusty road before a farmer came along, driving a cart loaded with sacks of grain. He gave her a ride right into Greenville.

A feeling of excitement gripped her as she walked along the streets of the town. Greenville, the county seat and a busy manufacturing center, seemed to pulse with life. She heard the loud screeching noise of a sawmill and, a little farther on, the great hum and clatter of a woodworking factory with its lathes and other power tools for fashioning barrel staves, tubs, pails, chairs and broom handles. Next she passed a broom factory. It was all so busy, so thrilling, so different from the quiet wilderness back home.

The wail of a steam whistle, followed by the ding-dong of a locomotive's bell, drew Annie's attention to the railroad station. One of the four trains that arrived daily in Greenville over the tracks of the Dayton & Union Railroad was puffing in. As Annie reached the station the train came to a stop with a hiss of steam and a muffled squeak of brakes.

She watched the dozen or so passengers alight from a string of coaches behind the engine. Three or four men threw their valises into a surrey alongside the station platform and got into it themselves. The driver clucked to his horses, and the vehicle moved off down the street with a clip-clop of hoofs. Where did they come from? Why had they come to Greenville? She wished she could talk to them and find out about the world of great cities. Annie continued on down the street. She passed the surrey from the station, which had drawn up in front of the local hotel.

Everything in this bustling town was exciting to Annie. Her wide-eyed gaze wandered up and down the street.

Then she saw a sign over a building informing all who

looked that this was the general store run by G. A. Katzenberger and his brother.

Annie tightened her grip on the string of game birds, shook off her fear and marched into the store. Inside, a bewildering assortment of goods and groceries met her eyes. The place had a tantalizing smell. There were cheeses, spicy strings of sausages that hung by the meat counter, the vinegary odor of pickles in a big barrel, the rich aroma of fresh-ground coffee, and the pungent one of tobacco and snuff.

A chubby man with blond hair and a fresh, rosy complexion, wearing a butcher's apron, stood behind the store's meat counter, serving a Greenville housewife. He was Charles Katzenberger, one of the store's proprietors. The scales clanked as he put a big slice of steak on them. Then he wrapped the meat in thick, shiny butcher's paper, reached up and grabbed the string hanging from a ball in a kind of metal cage overhead and pulled it down as he tied the package. He handed it to his customer and gave her the change from a dollar. As she left, Mr. Katzenberger turned to Annie. His blue eyes rested curiously on her string of birds. He seemed puzzled when she asked if he would buy them. He wanted to know who had bagged the grouse and quail. He could scarcely believe her answer.

Could Annie supply him with more game regularly? Annie assured him that she could. She left the store with money jingling in her pocket. She felt almost as if she were flying as she went on to her next stop—her plan was working!

Frenchy La Motte's little shop was crowded with a hodgepodge of things hunters and trappers could obtain in exchange for their furs and skins—ammunition for shotguns and rifles, traps, harnesses, saddles, axes, lanterns. Frenchy, a dark-eyed man with a red beard, came out of the back room where he sorted pelts into bundles. He looked suspiciously at Annie's skins. . . . Could the child have stolen them? But he took her pelts and paid her, partly in money, along with a good supply of bullets.

Jubilantly, Annie headed for home. From then on, her days were full ones. Frenchy La Motte took all the skins she could bring in. And Charles Katzenberger found a ready market for her grouse and quail with Greenville housewives.

But soon Annie was bringing in more game than Mr. Katzenberger could sell. He admired her energy and industry and wanted to find a larger market for the extra game. He talked with the carrier who drove up from Cincinnati with Greenville's mail. What would he charge to carry some game birds to the city and sell them to the manager of the Bevis House Hotel, John Frost?

The mailman soon brought word that John Frost would be glad to take some of Annie's grouse and quail for the hotel dining room. Frost was so pleased with what Annie sent that he took all the extra birds she could supply. Soon the mortgage on Joseph Shaw's farm was paid off.

Meanwhile, Annie had changed her name again. She couldn't forget how she had been tormented at the county home by the youngsters. Annie was now substantially the head of the household, and the others went along with her plan to change the family name to the rather odd one of "Mozee" —except for her brother John, who insisted on keeping the old name for himself.

When Annie was fifteen her sister Lyda and Lyda's husband, Joe Stein, invited her to come to Cincinnati and live with them. Although Annie's going would mean the end of the extra income that made the family prosperous, her mother thought only of what it would mean to her daughter. In Cincinnati Annie could at last go to school regularly and get a proper education.

So Annie went to Cincinnati. Lyda and Joe welcomed her eagerly. Until then Greenville had seemed like a great metropolis to the young girl. Now it faded into insignificance beside one of the largest cities in America, known as the Queen City of the West.

Cincinnati's gaiety and liveliness dazzled her. Everything about it was on a grand scale. Until then she hadn't realized that so many people could be packed into one place. She gazed in wonderment at the big hotels, especially the Burnet House—the grandest one in America, Lyda boasted. Looking at the huge bulk of the Music Hall, Annie didn't doubt that it took eight thousand people to fill all the seats. Pike's Opera House, where stage plays were performed, awed her with its magnificence. She marveled when Lyda and Joe described the Coliseum, a place where you could dine while you watched a variety show.

Nor was the Coliseum the only place in Cincinnati where you could enjoy an excellent meal. There were restaurants all over the city. The Steins told Annie that no other place in America could rival it for genuine German cooking. So many Germans had settled in Cincinnati when they came over from Europe that it was like a piece of Germany transported across the Atlantic Ocean.

Along the great bend in the Ohio River that formed the city's southern boundary Annie saw big steamboats, driven by huge paddle wheels, coming alongside or leaving the wharves on the waterfront, their rails lined with passengers. Many of the travelers were people from the East, moving westward. Attracted by what they had read and heard of the Far West —its gold and silver mines, its vast cattle ranches on the grazing lands of the Great Plains—they saw it as a new and exciting land of opportunity. It might be dangerous with its Indians and desperadoes, but that didn't stop the tide of westward migration that had begun in 1848 with the start of the California gold rush.

Joe Stein told Annie that the steamboats plied to and from other big cities on the Ohio and Mississippi rivers, even as far away as New Orleans. She saw these and smaller riverboats loading or discharging freight, as well as canalboats drawn by mules plodding on the banks of the Miami Canal that connected Cincinnati with the region to the north. Joe Stein knew about the many materials and products the river steamers and canalboats carried. He spoke of sand, lumber, whiskey, beer, hay, corn and especially pork. Joe said that Cincinnati's stockyards provided so many hams and other meat products from hogs that the city had earned the name of "Porkopolis."

One day they all went up on the heights that fringed the city's northern edge, where Annie could see all of Cincinnati spread out before her. Lyda pointed to one area close to the river and said that she and Joe had considered living in one of the suburbs there—either Oakley or Hyde Park.

Oakley . . . Annie liked the way it sounded.

All along the heights were restaurants, beer gardens and pavilions where people dined, danced to the music of German bands playing waltzes or watched shooting exhibitions. Up there too were shooting galleries and the German Shooting Club.

When they came to Charlie Stuttelberger's shooting gallery, Joe suggested they go in. He liked to try his skill at the metal ducks and rabbits that paraded past on a moving track, challenging the shooter's aim. Joe fired six shots. Twice a gong sounded as two ducks fell over. Then Joe handed the rifle to Annie and told her to try her luck; if she could score five hits out of six shots there would be no charge.

Annie pumped out the six shots in quick succession. The gong rang six times so rapidly that it sounded like a fire alarm. Joe Stein's mouth sagged open. Charlie Stuttelberger, watching, blinked in amazement. He handed Annie another gun and told her to shoot again. Once more came the six shots with machine-gun speed and the clang-clang-clang-clang-clang-clang of the gong.

Stuttelberger asked Annie where she had learned to shoot like that. She told him she shot grouse and quail for Mr. Frost's hotel right there in Cincinnati. Stuttelberger knew that Frank Butler, who did exhibition shooting at the Coliseum, was staying at Jack Frost's Bevis House. He told Annie he wanted to take her and the Steins over to meet Frost.

At the hotel Mr. Frost recognized Annie's name at once. He had good reason to remember. Most hunters shot game birds with a shotgun, and people who ordered quail or grouse in restaurants were accustomed, as they ate, to spitting out the pellets used as ammunition for shotguns. Guests in Jack Frost's dining room were not bothered with pellets and they appreciated it. The birds supplied by the girl up in Darke County were always shot through the head with a rifle bullet.

Charlie Stuttelberger told Jack Frost he would bet fifty dollars on Annie if a match with Frank Butler could be arranged. Frost said he would ask Butler. Shortly afterward, Annie and the Steins were summoned to the German Shooting Club. Butler had agreed to the match.

Frank Butler was a big, smiling, handsome man with blue eyes and a ruddy complexion. He wore a shooting coat with a belt and a soft green hat with a jaunty feather in it. He carried the shotgun he used in his act at the Coliseum. Butler stared when he saw Annie. This must be a joke Jack Frost was playing on him. He'd been told he was to shoot against a girl, but this child . . . .

He soon found out it was no joke. It was to be a trapshooting match with shotguns, firing at clay discs called pigeons that were sent whirling into the air by a powerful spring. A coin was tossed, and Butler won the right to shoot first. He called "Pull" to the trap operator, and the first clay bird sailed up. As he fired, the disc disappeared in a cloud of dust. Then it was Annie's turn. Her shot also smashed the bird.

In succession, Butler and Annie each broke twenty-four discs. Then Butler missed his twenty-fifth shot. Annie didn't hesitate an instant, but raised her gun and fired, breaking the bird as it flew upward. She had won over a professional marksman.

The spectators could hardly believe what they had seen. Even Charlie Stuttelberger, in spite of his confidence in Annie's skill, wouldn't have been surprised to lose the fifty dollars he had bet on her. Annie herself was calm. She knew her ability, and this self-confidence carried her through to victory.

Frank Butler did not feel humiliated or resentful about his loss to Annie. He became a constant caller at the Steins' house, and on June 22, 1876, he and Annie were married.

Frank was ten years older than Annie. He had been born in

Ireland in 1850. The years of his boyhood were terrible ones for all the Irish people. Since they lived chiefly on potatoes, when these crops failed in the years from 1845 to 1847, terrible famines and hardships resulted that lasted for years afterward. Most of the land was owned by English landlords who evicted thousands of Irish farmers when they were unable to pay rent for the land they occupied. All over the country, miserable, starving people wandered about in rags. Thousands died. Sometimes children became separated from their parents and perished from winter cold and lack of food.

Frank Butler may have been one of these wretched children. He came to America alone at the age of thirteen, having worked his passage to New York aboard a ship. In New York he took various jobs to support himself: He drove a milk wagon, cleaned the stalls in livery stables, sold newspapers and worked for two years aboard a fishing boat.

He wanted something better. Trained-animal acts were popular in vaudeville theaters; so Frank bought a pair of dogs, trained them to do tricks and was able to get a few bookings at theaters in New York, Brooklyn and Philadelphia. Then he decided to learn trick shooting and mastered it by diligent practice. He teamed with another marksman, Billy Graham, and they were booked into theaters east of the Mississippi River. That was how he happened to be playing the Coliseum in Cincinnati when Annie came there.

Frank and Annie's marriage was a very happy one. Frank called her "Little Annie" or "Little Girl." For no apparent reason she called him "Jimmy." Frank ended his partnership with Billy Graham, and soon Frank and Annie were booked together for a theatrical tour. For her it meant another name change. She wanted something more attractive than "Mozee" for her billing with Frank. She remembered she had liked the name of Oakley, the Cincinnati suburb, so she and Frank became the team of Butler and Oakley.

As their shooting act traveled from city to city, eager audiences greeted them. There were few forms of entertainment available at that time—no radio or television, motion pictures or phonographs—and for the most part people amused themselves at home with simple pleasures. Many boys and girls learned to play the piano or some other musical instrument. Home concerts and dances were popular. People played games—chess, checkers, dominoes, cards. Since there were few public libraries except in large cities, people were more likely to have good-sized home libraries with books they had bought themselves. Theatrical attractions of all kinds drew large audiences, and vaudeville shows were especially in demand. People welcomed the chance to see the skills of expert jugglers, magicians, acrobats, animal trainers, comedians and dancers who appeared on theater bills.

Among the most popular vaudeville acts were those starring talented sharpshooters. Hitting a difficult target never failed to hold audiences spellbound. There were public shooting ranges all over the country and many fans in the audience knew and appreciated skill at marksmanship.

Also, people were attracted by the stories they had heard about gun duels in the Far West between desperadoes and sheriffs in the frontier towns. "Bad men" like Alf "Killer" Slade were famous as killers who stayed alive themselves because they were fast on the draw and crack shots with a revolver. Sheriffs and other lawmen like the noted "Wild Bill" Hickok and Wyatt Earp who captured such ruffians had their share of hero worship in the East and Middle West for the same reason. People admired and glorified both the good and bad expert shots.

Something that proved even more intriguing to vaudeville audiences was the sight of a dainty girl who hardly looked old enough to be out of grade school, drilling bullets through one target after another with never a miss. The public fell in love with Annie Oakley.

3

ANNIE'S CAREER IN SHOW BUSINESS BEGINS

The stage team of Butler and Oakley toured all over the Middle West. Like others in vaudeville they put up with a good many difficulties and discomforts. Hotels and actors' boardinghouses in the towns and cities where they played were too often dreary, and the menus in the restaurants and dining rooms were monotonous. Going from one place to another meant traveling by train, often overnight on bumpy roadbeds behind steam locomotives belching black and cinder-laden smoke that could never be quite shut out of the cars behind. Vaudeville actors were accustomed to changing their costumes in drafty, poorly furnished dressing rooms.

Nonetheless, Annie enjoyed herself. She thought that appearing on a theater stage before crowds of spectators was glamorous. It set her apart from ordinary people. Life off-stage might sometimes be tedious and ordinary, but the acclaim of audiences made up for all the inconveniences and gave her a thrilling taste of fame.

Frank Butler, a seasoned trouper, was able to coach Annie in the devices vaudeville actors used to make their acts pleasing to audiences. Annie was a skilled marksman; but Frank knew the knacks of trick shooting that always drew enthusiastic applause. Annie soon became as adept at these stage arts as her husband.

Annie and Frank were happy. Between shows, in their hotel room, Frank set to work to give his wife an education. He had taught himself by reading books, newspapers and magazines, and he was smart and quick to learn. Now he read to Annie. She too learned quickly, and eventually was as well educated as many people who had attended school regularly.

Perhaps the Butlers would have been content to go on as vaudeville actors indefinitely but for a big, bald-headed man with a beard and mustache who came to their dressing room one day in 1884. He introduced himself as Lewis Sells. The Butlers were thrilled. Their caller's name stood for the Sells Brothers Circus, which was advertised as "The Biggest of All Big Shows." Big it was, filling three long railroad trains when it moved from one place to another. Under its main tent—the big top—human and animal performers appeared in the one hundred acts that went on in its three rings daily.

Mr. Sells's chief interest in the Butlers was in Annie. He asked questions: Could she do in a circus ring the tricks she did on theater stages? Could she shoot from a horse's back as she rode around the ring? She told him she could. Sells nodded and drew from his pocket a contract for the Butlers to appear for forty weeks in the Sells Brothers Circus. The billing, he said, would be Oakley and Butler.

They signed the contract. The circus appealed to them with its glitter and romance. Also, with the Sells Brothers Circus they would play before much larger audiences and thus become better known. Frank Butler didn't mind that his wife's name would come before his in the billing. He never showed any jealousy because of her superior skill with a gun. He knew Annie was a better shot and that the novelty of a diminutive female sharpshooter was especially popular.

The Butlers joined the circus immediately. It was the end of Frank's part in their shooting act. He became Annie's manager and assistant. When she rode into the ring for her act Frank would have her shooting table ready, her guns loaded and laid out with the rest of the equipment she used. Then, as she galloped around the ring, he would toss the targets into the air.

Annie Oakley was such an immediate success with the Sells Brothers Circus that the owners hoped to make a big profit by keeping the show playing during the winter of 1884–85 in the mild weather of New Orleans. The World's Fair and Cotton Centennial Exposition opened there in December at Audubon Park. The circus tent went up in a field just beyond the park. A special spur line was laid from the main railroad line to the exposition site. Of course the circus would get its share of the thousands of visitors to the fair.

But early in January 1885 it began to rain in New Orleans. Day after day rain fell. It turned the exposition grounds and the circus lot into fields of mud. The expected crowds never came.

For the Sells Brothers Circus the bad weather was a calamity. The ticket sellers at the entrance had nothing to do and the tiers of seats under the big top were empty. There was no money to pay the performers, and the show was halted with only the desperate hope that better weather would make it possible to reopen.

To Annie and Frank the future seemed as dreary as the muddy field where the circus was stalled and its people sloshed about. The two had found life with the Sells Brothers Circus somewhat less romantic than it had appeared at first. Their accommodations on the road in vaudeville, while dreary, were better than a circus tent, and they were used to performing with a roof over their heads in theaters. They were still not fully accustomed to living and working under canvas in a tent show. Now, in such a long spell of rain as New Orleans was experiencing, it was impossible to avoid disagreeable dampness; it was a rather unpleasant experience. And Annie's position as a star also suffered. At the Sells Brothers Circus something was always going on in all three rings under the big top. So while Annie's shooting act was a featured one, it did not get as much attention from audiences as she and Frank had attracted in their vaudeville act.

Over at the Metairie Racetrack another tent show had set up its equipment. One day Frank Butler suggested to Annie that they go and have a look at Buffalo Bill's Wild West. Perhaps, just perhaps, in spite of the rain, it might be doing better business than Sells Brothers.

But when they reached the racetrack it was all mud and black pools of water. Down at one end of the grandstand they saw several soggy-looking Indians squatting in front of tepees, trying to coax some heat out of smoky fires. Up in the grandstand a lone man was sitting, smoking a cigar. Annie and Frank sloshed through the mud and climbed up to him.

The one occupant of the seats looked prosperous enough. He was a big, imposing man with a luxuriant beard and mustache and long hair that flowed down to his shoulders from under a broad-brimmed hat. He wore a Prince Albert, the long, double-breasted frock coat then in style, and striped trousers.

Major John Burke, the show's publicity man, or "advance" man, was not feeling prosperous, in spite of his fine clothes. He had been brooding over the Wild West's money troubles. One of the most serious was that the show's marksman had left. Burke showed no enthusiasm as he looked at his visitors. If they were looking for jobs they had better go elsewhere.

They introduced themselves: Mr. and Mrs. Frank Butler of the Sells Brothers Circus. Frank said they had come over to the racetrack because there were certain things about their show that they didn't like. They had heard conditions were better with Buffalo Bill's Wild West. All this didn't bring a flicker of interest to Burke's face. But he began to listen more attentively when Butler said they were the greatest sharpshooting team in America.

Burke's gaze was fixed on Annie. She wasn't beautiful, but there was something else about her—a charm that he felt strongly as he studied her. If this tiny girl could shoot as well as her husband claimed she might be a great attraction in his show. Burke wished he could make the Butlers an offer, but it was impossible, with the Wild West unable to pay the performers it already had.

He told them how things stood. Rain and cold during a New England tour meant small audiences and had put the show about sixty thousand dollars in debt. It had continued to lose money when it moved westward and came down the Ohio and Mississippi Rivers on a riverboat, stopping along the way to give performances. Then, below Vicksburg, Mississippi, the steamer had been in a collision, and all of the show's buffalo and steers and much of the equipment had been lost.

Now the rain had destroyed any chance of recovering from these disastrous financial setbacks during the show's stand in New Orleans.

But things were bound to improve, said Burke, once they were on the road again. Would the Butlers come back to see him a month later, in Louisville, Kentucky?

The Butlers said they'd think it over and then went back through the mud to the Sells Brothers lot. They talked it over and decided to do what Burke suggested.

When Annie and Frank reached Louisville on April 24, 1885, they went to the ball park on the Ohio River where the big top and the show's smaller tents were pitched. The place seemed deserted. Everyone was downtown for the morning street parade. When Major Burke returned, he immediately took them to the show's target range.

While Annie was demonstrating her skill, Nate Salsbury, a partner in the Wild West, came along. He watched with satisfaction while Annie scored bull's-eye after bull's-eye. Then he asked Annie to be ready, in costume, for that afternoon's performance. Annie agreed, and they all went to the cook tent for lunch.

During lunch Annie looked up to see a tall, handsome man with dark eyes, a pointed beard and a mustache approaching the table. He wore a fringed jacket and a silk neckerchief fastened with a diamond stickpin. When Salsbury presented him to Annie, Buffalo Bill bowed gallantly, sweeping off his broad-brimmed Stetson hat to reveal his long, luxuriant hair. When he spoke to Annie for the first time he called her "Missie," his special name for her which he used from then on. Buffalo Bill then summoned the rest of the Wild West people to meet Annie. They must have seemed a bit frightening to her. The cowboys were a boisterous lot, young fellows used to the rough life of the western cattle ranges, and the Indians (the first Annie had ever met) were made to look particularly fierce. She was the only white woman in the show, and Buffalo Bill took pains to reassure her that she had nothing to fear from anyone in the Wild West. Introducing her, he told them all that he wanted them to like her and treat her well. They never failed to do so.

From then on Buffalo Bill became the guiding force in Annie's extraordinary career. Years later she would write: "He was the kindest, simplest, most loyal man I ever knew.... the staunchest friend ...."

In contrast to the rain and mud and the empty stands in New Orleans, the sun shone warmly on a perfect spring afternoon, and the big top was jammed with spectators on the day of Annie's first appearance in Buffalo Bill's Wild West. The ringmaster strode into the center ring. In the flowery language of all circus ringmasters he bellowed Annie's introduction as the foremost woman sharpshooter in the world—"the little girl of the western plains, Annie Oakley!"

BUFFALO BILL
AND THE WILD WEST

Circuses had been popular in the United States ever since they first appeared in the 1820s. Throughout the country it was considered a great event when the circus came to town. People would get up before dawn to see the wagons arrive and to watch the roustabouts set up the circus tents. These husky fellows would put on an act of their own, forming a circle and swinging their mallets one after the other in perfect sequence as they drove the tent stakes into the ground. Small boys would be on hand early, too, hoping to be allowed to lug pails of water for the elephants in return for passes to the afternoon performance.

Schools usually were closed on the day the circus was in town. In the morning everyone went downtown to see the street parade with its clowns, acrobats, jugglers, chariot racers, wild animals and other attractions. In the afternoon the big top would be crowded with spectators of all ages.

Buffalo Bill and the Wild West

Buffalo Bill's Wild West show was a new kind of circus that took advantage of the tremendous interest in the settlement of the Far West among people throughout the East and Midwest.

Western expansion in America began not long after the end of the American Revolution. Many inhabitants of the thirteen colonies that originally formed the new nation began to look westward beyond the Allegheny Mountains for places in which they might start new settlements. They were pioneers —restless, adventurous men and women who felt that the original states were becoming overcrowded.

Naturally the Indians who lived on the lands west of the mountains objected. They knew how the tribes in the American colonies had gradually been pushed out of their villages and hunting grounds. The tribes of the lands in what are now Ohio and Indiana decided to fight the white men rather than suffer the same fate.

In 1794 the famous Revolutionary general "Mad Anthony" Wayne was sent by the government of the new nation to western Ohio. He and his one thousand soldiers defeated about two thousand Shawnee, Delaware, Wyandot and Miami Indian warriors at the battle of Fallen Timbers. The Indians were forced to yield all of southwestern Ohio and southeastern Indiana to the United States, and this area was then opened to settlement.

More of the American West was opened in 1803 with the Louisiana Purchase, by which President Thomas Jefferson obtained from France more than eight hundred twenty-five thousand square miles of the vast Mississippi Valley.

Buffalo Bill, born William Frederick Cody, was himself a product of this period of westward expansion. His family, like thousands of others, left home back east to head westward into the new land of opportunity in the Mississippi Valley. The Codys settled in Iowa and there, in 1846, William was born. When Will Cody was three years old he and his parents moved from Iowa to Salt Creek, Kansas, near Fort Leavenworth. Kansas was part of the huge territory (including all of California, New Mexico, Nevada and Utah as well as most of Arizona and part of Colorado) that had just been ceded to the United States following its victory in the Mexican War in 1848. Fort Leavenworth was the supply base for army posts in these new lands, and Cody's father, Isaac, made a living by supplying the garrison at the fort with hay and wood.

In 1857, when Will was eleven, Isaac Cody died, and the boy decided to go to work. His mother pleaded with him to stay in school, but he had always hated it. He got a job as a herder with the wagon trains that left Fort Leavenworth with supplies for distant army posts to the west. He had charge of forty or fifty oxen in the rear of the train that were used as replacements along the trails.

Cody loved this rugged life. He met Sioux, Cheyenne, Arapaho and other Indian chiefs and warriors, as well as some of the scouts and Indian fighters. One of the most celebrated of the scouts was Kit Carson, whom Cody admired so much that he named his own son Kit Carson Cody.

By 1860 the small western settlements, trading posts and mining camps had grown tremendously. More and more pioneers arrived every day. The old method of delivering mail by wagon train was no longer adequate, and to meet the demand for faster service the Pony Express was started. Will Cody became one of its riders.

Pony Express riders were not allowed to weigh more than

one hundred thirty-five pounds, and they could only carry thirteen pounds of equipment, including a knife and revolver and saddlebag filled with mail that cost five dollars a half-ounce in postage. They had the swiftest, strongest ponies that money could buy and rode at full gallop, changing horses every ten miles, along seventy-five- to one-hundred-mile sectors of the nearly two thousand miles of the Pony Express route from St. Joseph, Missouri, to Sacramento, California.

As a Pony Express rider, Cody saw a great deal of the Far West and witnessed many of the great changes that took place there in the years after the Mexican War treaty had opened the area to full settlement. Salt Lake City, the major stop on the Pony Express route, had grown from a collection of log cabins put up by Mormon pioneers to a flourishing city of about ten thousand inhabitants. From there the rough and rocky road used by stagecoaches coming from St. Joseph became merely a blazed trail that passed through the arid desert badlands of Utah and Nevada until it reached Carson City, which had been started as a trading post in 1851 and had also grown rapidly. Then the route surmounted the rugged peaks of the Sierra Nevada mountain range and reached its end at Sacramento, California's capital. Sacramento too had grown with remarkable speed since its establishment as a colony under the Mexican government in 1839. Its founder, a Swiss citizen named John Augustus Sutter, owned a mill on the American River where gold was discovered in 1848. This set off the famous gold rush of 1849. Sacramento was the jumping-off place for the thousands of prospectors who flocked to California.

After the Civil War began, Cody enlisted in the Union Army. He saw no fighting, but served in a cavalry regiment in

Kansas. He was still a private when the war ended; but afterward, while serving with the 5th U.S. Cavalry at Fort Hays, Kansas, as chief of scouts, he was given the pay of a colonel. He took that title, even though he had no official officer's rank, and he used it for the rest of his life.

Life in the Far West seemed wildly romantic and dangerously exciting to people back east. They were thrilled by the adventures and exploits of rough-riding, sharpshooting heroes like Wild Bill Hickok, who had killed many outlaws during his career as a scout and law-enforcement officer. Cody himself became famous in the East. Ned Buntline, a New York writer of dime novels, paperback books that were tremendously popular at that time, decided that Cody would make an ideal character for a "Western"—by far the favorite kind of dime novel on the market.

After that, Cody, under the name of Buffalo Bill, was featured in Buntline's stories as a great scout, hunter and killer of desperadoes and Indians. The nickname was well chosen, because thousands of buffalo then roamed the Great Plains.

The lure of the buffalo for eastern hunters enabled Cody to make a great deal of money and to become even more famous. General Philip Sheridan, in command at Fort Hays, asked him to be the guide for a party of rich sportsmen from New York City on a buffalo-hunting expedition. A special train from New York brought the party west to Nebraska, where Buffalo Bill met them.

He gave them their money's worth. They were made to feel that they were in country where danger lurked everywhere—killers who would shoot a man on sight if they didn't like his looks, savage Indians always on the warpath with tomahawks and scalping knives, and fierce wild animals. Actually the "dudes" were as safe and as well provided for as they were in the drawing rooms of their New York mansions. Ahead of the mounted party a hundred troops fanned out in all directions. In case of accident, four ambulance wagons followed the cavalcade. They also bore the guns the hunters would use and provided a comfortable ride for any of the party who became tired of sitting on a horse. In the rear were supply trains loaded with food, wine and ice.

The herds of buffalo on the plains were rapidly being exterminated by such hunters. It didn't take an expert to bring down a buffalo. The big, shaggy animals didn't charge quickly. The eastern hunters shot scores of them and left them to rot.

At night the easterners lounged around the campfire, drinking wine and listening to Buffalo Bill's tales of adventure.

Other parties came. Cody scared the wits out of one group by staging an attack by some Pawnee Indians, whom he and his men drove off. When his spreading fame reached Europe a titled English sportsman crossed the Atlantic with some of his friends to enjoy a buffalo hunt. Then, in 1871, Grand Duke Alexis of Russia came to New York. He fancied himself a hunter, and through General Sheridan a trip aboard a special train to North Platte, Nebraska, was arranged for the duke and his party. American newspapers carried headlines about the trip, playing up its guide, the famous scout, Buffalo Bill.

Although buffalo were such easy targets, the duke proved to be a miserable shot. After Cody got him into position for an easy kill, he missed twelve shots before he was maneuvered so close to his quarry that he couldn't possibly fail to bring the animal down. Nevertheless, when the Russian newspapers later reported the incident, they heralded the nobleman's triumph.

New York newspaper publisher James Gordon Bennett and

others who had hunted with Cody sent him five hundred dollars in cash, a railroad pass and an invitation to come east.

In New York City Cody's hosts put him up at the exclusive Union League Club. He wore the expensive "dude's duds" they bought him, including a full-dress suit for formal social affairs, but he wisely insisted on wearing his broadbrimmed Stetson hat and refused to let a barber cut his long hair. Thus all who saw him were reminded that this was the daring western scout and Pony Express rider.

For five weeks Cody was royally entertained, attending many social events and increasing his fame still more. Then a telegram from General Sheridan summoned him back west to become chief scout for the 3rd Cavalry. Soon afterward his neighbors in and around his home near Fort McPherson, Nebraska, put his name on the ballot as a candidate for the Nebraska Legislature, but Buffalo Bill wasn't interested in politics, and although he was elected, he never took his seat.

Ned Buntline planned to produce a play about the wild West. Shows featuring outlaws, Indians, scouts and cowboys were already becoming popular in eastern theaters. Buntline asked Cody to appear in his play, and Buffalo Bill set out to meet the writer in Chicago.

The play Buntline wrote was so dreadful that all the newspaper theatrical critics did their best to destroy it in their reviews. It didn't matter. When Buffalo Bill and his brave men came on stage to wipe out an attack by Indians (white actors made up as red men) the audience stood up and cheered. The critics in St. Louis, Cincinnati, Albany, Boston and finally New York unanimously agreed that this was one of the worst plays ever staged, but it played to capacity crowds.

The name "Buffalo Bill" was by now well known throughout the country, and it proved to be Cody's most valuable asset when, in 1883, he organized his wild West show. The show, featuring Indians, cowboys and their horses and Buffalo Bill himself, the last of the scouts and Indian fighters, captured the imagination of a public that was still fascinated by the romance of the Far West.

5

ANNIE'S EARLY DAYS
WITH
THE WILD WEST

By the time Annie Oakley joined the Wild West in 1885, the show's popularity had soared. As it moved west that summer, Annie soon realized that she was not just one of the acts in a circus but a star attraction.

She was accustomed, of course, to taking part in the morning street parades held when a circus arrived for a stand in town. But now, among the people lining the sidewalks along the parade route, craning their necks and oh-ing and ah-ing, all eyes were turned upon her. John Burke, arriving ahead of the show, always saw to it that the newspapers wrote stories about the show's thrilling new headliner, "The Little Girl of the Western Plains." This had quickly become one of Annie's nicknames, even though she had never been west of the Mississippi River.

Buffalo Bill, of course, drew admiring attention as he led the parade, a striking figure on his magnificent horse, doffing his hat to the onlookers. So did the bandwagon, loaded with musicians playing a march while just behind, six white horses stepped along in time to the music. Pawnee Indian braves came next, mounted on broncos and led by their chief, White Eagle, resplendent in a headdress of eagle feathers; then Chief Dave and his Wichita tribesmen, followed by mounted Mexican cowboys—*vaqueros*—their spurs jingling. All received their share of recognition; but always the spectators' applause turned to cheers when Annie came riding along in a carriage drawn by a team of matched mustangs. Something about the tiny girl with her bewitching smile never failed to captivate those who saw her. In the parade she wore a feminine-style Stetson hat, a blouse covered with medals, a pleated skirt and gaiters.

Annie loved every bit of her new life. When she performed in the arena she played to packed stands. She was constantly delighted by the tremendous public response to her and the Wild West. She liked the show's people and they liked her. She was comfortable in the quarters Buffalo Bill had provided for her and Frank Butler: an A-frame tent next to the one he and Nate Salsbury occupied. It had two folding cots, canvas chairs, a table and a collapsible bathtub, all set on a wooden floor covered with an Axminster rug.

At this time Major Burke left the show on a mission to Fort Yates in the Dakota Territory, where he picked up two Sioux Indian interpreters. From there he traveled south to a Sioux reservation on the Grand River, where Sitting Bull, chief of the most powerful Sioux tribe, the Hunkpapas, lived. Sitting Bull had been the leader of the Indians at the Battle of Little Big Horn when General Custer and all of his men were killed.

Sitting Bull was well named, for he was built like a bull,

with massive shoulders and a large head. The fierce expression on his face, pitted with the scars left by smallpox, did justice to his reputation. Burke was sure that Sitting Bull would be a sensational attraction for the Wild West Show.

After long deliberation the chief agreed to come east and join the Wild West. At his first performance Sitting Bull came into the arena mounted on a horse. He wore a brocaded waistcoat, black trousers, beaded moccasins, a bright red tie and big crucifix on a chain around his neck. But the spectators saw only the Indian who had massacred an American general and every one of his American soldiers, and they booed the chief. Sitting Bull left the ring scowling. He wanted no more of this; he would go home to Dakota.

Just then Annie Oakley galloped in. The chief stopped, watching her smash target after target. As she finished her act, Sitting Bull gave a shout of approval and followed her to the door of her tent. There he called out in the Sioux language: "Little Straight Shooter! Little Sure-Shot!"

This small girl, so skilled with her gun, had captivated the old chief. It was more than just admiration for her talent; he became quite fond of her, "adopting" her as his daughter, and this friendship may have influenced his decision to stay with the show for the rest of the season.

After performances in New England towns the show moved into Canada. There, in Montreal and cities in Ontario, Sitting Bull's appearances were more enjoyable for him. Unlike the Americans, the Canadian spectators had no reason to be loyal to General Custer and his soldiers. As they saw it, the massacre had simply been a battle in which each side either had to kill the enemy or be killed themselves. The Indians had won, and the Canadians applauded their leader.

Annie was as fond of Sitting Bull as he was of her. But although she liked his honesty she did not understand or approve of his unusual generosity. While his salary of fifty dollars a week was high for those days, he had little of it left after he had sent some home to his two wives and then had given most of the rest to poor newsboys and bootblacks who hung around the circus grounds.

Annie, according to Dexter Fellows, the famous circus publicity man who joined the Wild West later on, was rather miserly. When the other troupers with the show took advantage of a day off to go together for a holiday in town, she seldom joined them, Fellows said. Also, he didn't approve of her going to Cody's tent each day to fill her small pitcher with lemonade from the big one provided for him. And he claimed that while she would join others in a glass of beer, this was only when someone else was paying for it.

Fellows may have had the wrong impression of her frugality. It could have been due to the poverty in which she grew up, making her careful about spending money for trifles. Annie was always generous with her family. Once she began to make a good salary, she and Frank sent money home regularly so that a new living room for the Darke County cabin could be built and furnished and some new things added to the kitchen.

The show returned to the United States and played in midwestern cities until October, when it ended the season in St. Louis. Then its people went their different ways, and the equipment and animals went into winter quarters.

When the show closed for the winter, Annie and Frank Butler made a trip back to the farmhouse in Darke County. For Annie it was a homecoming. Her mother, stepfather and

Emily Brumbaugh, her half sister, welcomed the Butlers to a house that was bigger and more comfortable than when Annie had left it, because of the money the Butlers had sent.

Annie loved it all. The woods and fields outside were beautiful under their white blanket of snow; inside, the house was snug, warmed by crackling log fires in the stove and fireplace. The family, and neighbors who came in, listened breathlessly to Annie's accounts of Buffalo Bill, the show and its people, and pored over her scrapbook with its many newspaper clippings.

It was especially nice for Annie to be able to share her success with people who knew how far she had gone from the poverty and unhappiness of her childhood.

There was no time for boredom all through that winter in the wilderness. Although Annie lived in a new world, she thoroughly enjoyed revisiting the old one. She studied the books she had brought with her—reading, geography, history and spelling. While she read and practiced her spelling, her hands were busy with her needle, sewing or doing embroidery. By the time spring came she had a whole new set of costumes for her act in the Wild West.

Frank was happy, too. He and Annie tramped through the snowy woods hunting for quail, rabbits and squirrels for the table. Frank spent the long winter evenings reading, writing letters or turning out humorous or sentimental verses that, if not great poetry, were enjoyed by all the family.

6

NEW TRIUMPHS

By spring, when a letter arrived summoning them to St. Louis for the start of the show's 1886 season, Annie and Frank were ready to go. There they found that the Wild West had become considerably larger. A good share of the show's profits during the 1885 season had gone into improvements. There were more Indians, cowboys, ring performers, roustabouts, teamsters, horses and buffalo. Under the big top an enormous panorama of mountains and flat-topped mesas of the western ranges, painted on canvas stretched over a wooden framework, provided a background for the performers in the rings, especially for a new spectacle, "Custer's Massacre." Another new feature was the appearance of two cowgirls in a pony race. Sitting Bull had decided to go home to the Dakota reservation, and his place was taken by two other chiefs, American Horse and Rocky Bear.

The Wild West filled twenty-six railroad cars when the

show moved out of St. Louis to cities in Indiana, Ohio, West Virginia and Maryland and to Washington, D.C. When the show left Washington for Philadelphia, Annie had an agonizing pain in her right ear. Nevertheless, she obeyed the rule of show business: "The show must go on." Somehow she finished her first performance. Back in their tent, Frank rinsed out the infected ear with warm water and Castile soap. The cause of the trouble fell into the basin—a tiny insect.

The ear was still inflamed and very painful. She refused to go to a hospital, and continued on to the end of the Philadelphia performances. After the show moved north to Staten Island in New York City a doctor examined the ear. He told Annie she must remain absolutely quiet for three days. But after he left the pain stopped, and she got into her costume and joined the parade in Manhattan.

She was so sure her ordeal was over that she went for a ride on her pony that Sunday over the pretty country roads on Staten Island. The summer sun was hot, and when she returned she felt so faint that Frank had to help her dismount. Blood poisoning had set in, and the doctor had to lance her ear. She was delirious for three days with a raging fever. The next day she was back in the ring, shattering targets with perfect aim. She missed four performances, and these were the only ones she missed in the seventeen years she was with Buffalo Bill's Wild West.

Her insistence on resuming her act as soon as possible may have been motivated by something besides her iron will and self-reliance. On Staten Island a young woman named Lillian Smith joined the show. She had begun shooting as a child of seven in California and she had ridden horses ever since she was able to stay seated in a saddle. On the bill she was headlined as "The California Huntress."

She could hit a tossed-up plate thirty times in fifteen seconds. During her act ten balls were hung on strings from a pole and swung rapidly around; she would break them all. And her aim at the glass balls that Annie also used was extraordinary; she had broken three hundred twenty-three of them without a miss. But Lillian was a rawboned girl without the gracefulness and appeal that had made Annie so popular. Nor did she have the imagination that enabled Annie to add so many winning little touches to her act. All that summer Annie used her charm to full advantage over her rival. It was another instance in which Annie's determination carried her to victory over any attempt to defeat her.

On Staten Island all that summer of 1886 the show had its greatest success so far. There were two performances a day—the afternoon one and another each evening, made possible by the installation of big electric arc lights. Huge crowds came from all over New York City, Brooklyn (then a separate city), northern New Jersey and towns along the Hudson River. People came for a day's outing, strolling through the little Indian village with its tepees and past the corral with its many broncos, ponies and larger horses and staring at the herd of buffalo. Some brought lunches to eat at refreshment areas on the grounds; others preferred dining at the excellent restaurant there while a military band played.

Many notables came for the show. They included Governor David Bennett Hill of New York State, from Albany; Mayor W. R. Grace of New York City; and Phineas T. Barnum, the most famous of all circus showpeople. The Barnum & Bailey Circus was indeed what its advertising claimed: "The Greatest Show on Earth." Cody's Wild West was a different kind of tent show with no need to try to rival the bigger one, and Mr. Barnum gave it well-deserved praise.

All summer Major Burke entertained newspapermen on the show lot. They knew perfectly well that some of his tales were exaggerations, but they printed them, realizing that their readers would enjoy them. Yet Annie Oakley was responsible for the best publicity the show received while it was on Staten Island.

One Sunday while she was out riding she came upon an orphanage. She stopped in and told them to send the children over to the show grounds as Annie Oakley's guests for a performance.

The next day fifty orphans arrived. Annie herself escorted them around before the show. When they trooped in to a special reserved section under the big top they were wide-eyed over what they had seen in the Indian village and corral. Now Buffalo Bill, Annie, Indians, cowboys and other performers held them spellbound.

Major Burke, fairly rubbing his hands over the opportunity for tremendous publicity that Annie had started, sent free tickets to every orphanage in New York City for "Annie Oakley Day." A horde of youngsters descended on the lot; by the time they left they were filled with wonder—and with popcorn, ice cream and pink lemonade. The publicity that resulted ensured that every seat would be occupied for the rest of the summer.

One other visitor to the Wild West gave Nate Salsbury a new idea. He was James Steele Mackaye, one of the great playwrights and theatrical producers of those days. Mackaye told Salsbury that he was greatly impressed with the show. In September, Salsbury wrote to ask Mackaye to stage the Wild West in New York City's Madison Square Garden during the coming winter.

This was a new triumph for the show. "Playing the Garden" was the great ambition of show producers, as well as of actors and actresses. The Wild West was to perform at the foremost playhouse in New York, the amusement capital of the United States.

New York, the biggest city in America at the time, with a population of over a million people, was a glittering place. At night its hotels, theaters and restaurants were brilliantly illuminated with electric lights. Trains drawn by steam locomotives roared above the city streets on elevated tracks. They whisked people from one part of the town to another at breath-taking speed. Below, the streets were jammed with the slower-moving horsecars.

For the rich, New York was a lavish playground. It had the best theatrical attractions, hotels, restaurants, shops. And right in the center of all this excitement was Madison Square Garden.

The first Madison Square Garden opened in 1880 along New York's Madison Square. It occupied what had previously been a railroad station. It was rebuilt into a sports and entertainment center, with space for a larger arena and seating for bigger audiences than regular theaters could accommodate. Its location was excellent, for there were many fine hotels and restaurants close by.

In late October of 1886 Buffalo Bill, Nate Salsbury, Major Burke and the Wild West, with all its employees, animals and equipment, arrived. Only its tents, which would not be needed, were missing. Annie and Frank Butler rented an apartment in Manhattan's exclusive residential district of Murray Hill. The Indians pitched their tepees on the grounds the show had occupied on Staten Island the year before. Cody, Salisbury and Burke were at a hotel near the Garden and the rest of the show people moved into rooming houses in the vicinity.

Nate Salsbury had hired James Steele Mackaye to stage the Wild West show for its all-important debut at the Garden. Mackaye was told to create something that would astound everyone—even the most sophisticated New Yorkers.

Mackaye had left St. Louis for New York as soon as possible. With him came Matt Morgan, an experienced sign painter and illustrator who had an extremely vivid imagination. Although a horse show was playing at the Garden when the two men arrived, they began working immediately—staying late each night waiting for the show to be over—to construct a mammoth backdrop out of fifteen thousand square yards of canvas and many huge coils of rope and wire. Morgan painted a vast panorama of the Bad Lands of Dakota and Wyoming— ridges and mesas with fantastic shapes and brilliant colors. He used a tremendous amount of paint for this.

Mackaye agreed that this would be a spectacle that would impress even the most blasé easterners. Then Morgan decided to reproduce one of the cyclones that often blast over the Great Plains. A mechanic constructed a huge fan, connected with a wind tunnel, leading to the Garden's stage. Wagons were sent up to Westchester County, north of the city. They returned loaded with dry leaves and bits of underbrush that the big fan could whip into a whirling cloud. It worked, and Matt Morgan had his cyclone.

It was an ideal time for the show's opening. On October 28 of that year, the Statue of Liberty, the gift of France to the United States, had been dedicated. Standing in New York harbor, it welcomed hordes of immigrants arriving in America. It was a symbol of the land of freedom that would be their new home. Tourists from all over the country and the world would be coming to New York that fall to see the great statue, and they would flock to the Wild West show.

For weeks before the show opened, Major Burke was busy making front-page news about the Wild West's coming appearance. His efforts paid off, for all of Madison Square Garden's nine thousand seats were filled on opening night. The audience was amazed as the curtain went up on the circus arena with its sensational Bad Lands backdrop. It was indeed the perfect setting for all the features of the program, including Annie Oakley's performance. Buffalo Bill himself introduced her: "The Wild West presents the lovely lass of the western plains, Little Sure-Shot, the one and only Annie Oakley!"

Annie galloped in on a spotted pony, a trim, dainty, striking sight in the ring, with the mountains in the backdrop towering over her. Wearing a flowered deerskin jacket and fringed skirt, she rode swiftly and gracefully around the ring, shooting down, one after another, the targets that another rider threw into the air. Annie's act had been expanded and improved since she had first joined the Wild West. She had added many new stunts. In one she would leap off her mount to the tanbark floor of the ring, seize a rifle from a gun stand, raise it and pulverize five glass balls that Frank Butler had tossed into the air. In another, Frank whirled a glass ball on a string and Annie, aiming with a mirror, would break it. In other new stunts she would send a dime spinning from between two of Frank's fingers and would shoot cigarettes from his mouth and apples from the head of her pet poodle.

Another stunt that never failed to get applause was to send a bullet through a playing card held edgewise in Frank's hand at a distance of thirty paces. Annie also shot bullets through the spots on playing cards. She and Frank devised a special card about five by two inches with a picture of Annie on one side and a heart-shaped bull's-eye on the other, which she would puncture neatly with a bullet. These cards would be thrown to the audience when her act was over. Because free passes to shows were punched with holes by ticket takers, passes became known as Annie Oakleys, as they are often still called today.

At the conclusion of her act, Annie made a neat little curtsey to the audience and ran quickly into the wings of the stage. Madison Square Garden rocked to a thunderous burst of applause. In spite of Matt Morgan's cyclone, Buffalo Bill's appearance, expert riders on violently bucking broncos, Indians in battle dress and war paint who put on demonstrations of attacks on settlers of the Great Plains and all the other outstanding performances, Annie Oakley was the show's greatest star. Sellout crowds gave her frenzied applause, and for the first time Buffalo Bill showed signs of jealousy. His expression as he watched Annie's act became peevish. After the show he would often act sulky and ill-tempered. Whether Annie noticed Cody's petulance and suspected the reason is not known, but his jealousy was there. Buffalo Bill may have loved Annie like a daughter, but he was a vain man.

Certainly Cody's jealousy did not interfere with Annie's enjoyment of New York. Living and working in Manhattan marked a new pinnacle in her career. Annie enjoyed the opulence and excitement of New York and was dazzled by the famous people she and Frank met there.

She hated to leave, but the show finally closed on February 22, and Annie and Frank headed back to Darke County for a short visit. She was looking forward to spring, for Nate Salsbury planned to take the show to Europe to perform at Queen Victoria's Golden Jubilee. Under Victoria's rule the British Empire had spread over the entire globe, so vast a realm that it was said that "the sun never sets on the British Empire." All over the empire during 1887 there would be celebrations of Victoria's fifty-year reign, with the biggest of them all taking place in London, the British capital and at that time the largest city in the world. Nate Salsbury saw in the Jubilee an opportunity to expand the show's renown, bringing the sights and scenes of America's Far West to Europe for the first time.

LEFT: Annie Oakley (*Culver Pictures*). ABOVE: The busy levee at Cincinnati (*Culver Pictures*). RIGHT: Annie and Frank Butler (*The Bettmann Archive*).

ABOVE: Annie at a shooting match in Cincinnati (*The Bettmann Archive*). LEFT: Three views of Annie's Wild West performance (*Culver Pictures*).

ABOVE: Nate Salsbury and Buffalo Bill Cody (*Culver Pictures*).
RIGHT: Buffalo Bill and Sitting Bull (*The Bettmann Archive*).

TOP LEFT: A typical Wild West street parade *(Culver Pictures)*. BOTTOM LEFT: Buffalo Bill rescues a stagecoach in a scene from the Wild West Show *(The Bettmann Archive)*. ABOVE: Madison Square Garden *(Culver Pictures)*.

ABOVE: The Wild West Show departs for England (*Culver Pictures*). BELOW: A command performance for Queen Victoria (*Culver Pictures*).

Annie and the Butler's dog, Dave *(The Bettmann Archive)*.

7

EUROPE

Annie Oakley's world was changing. American isolation was ending and Annie kept pace with America's progress; she, like the country, went international.

Buffalo Bill's Wild West sailed to London in the steamer *State of Nebraska*, an appropriate name, since Cody's permanent home was near North Platte, Nebraska. It was a large ship, with accommodations for all the show's people and plenty of space belowdecks for the animals and equipment. Over two hundred passengers would be making the voyage, including nearly a hundred Indians, and one hundred sixty horses, eighteen buffalo and smaller numbers of Texas steers, mules and donkeys.

The pier in New York was a scene of busy confusion in the last days of March. Winches rumbled as the items needed to set up the Wild West in London were hoisted aboard. Most of the animals were driven up a gangway into the vessel's 'tween-decks hold, where stalls for them had been constructed. Getting the hulking buffalo aboard was not so easy. They had to be lifted in cargo nets and lowered to their stalls.

It had not been easy, either, to coax the Indians to make the voyage. They were superstitious and feared an Indian legend that if any of their race crossed the "Big Water" they would die. None of them did die, however, either during the voyage or in England.

The *State of Nebraska* sailed on March 31. Frank Butler was seasick and stayed in his cabin for two days. Annie proved to be a much better sailor. As the ship rolled and pitched in a storm, she had coffee with the captain in the chartroom. She stayed up on the bridge all day, fascinated to see how the ship was handled in the trough of heavy seas.

After eleven days at sea, the *State of Nebraska* arrived in London. The Wild West set up its tents at the Earl's Court Exhibition Grounds in the city's West End. The show didn't open until May 9, but its performers were kept busy giving interviews to reporters and going on sightseeing tours to the royal palaces, Buckingham, Kensington and St. James's; the Houses of Parliament with their clock tower where Big Ben tolled the hours in its deep-toned voice; Westminster Abbey; the Tower of London; and other famous places. Major Burke had made sure that the show's chief performers would be recognized as they went about; all over the city large posters with pictures of Buffalo Bill, Annie Oakley and the rest of the principal performers were displayed.

Europeans had long been fascinated by the exciting and fantastic stories about cowboys and Indians that had been published overseas. Many of them thought that such characters could be seen on the streets of every town and city in the

United States. Now that a show had arrived whose performers included some of these extraordinary Americans, Englishmen were eager to have a look at them.

Distinguished visitors came to the showgrounds before the opening date. On April 28, William Ewart Gladstone, one of England's great prime ministers, appeared at the showgrounds with his wife. After meeting them, Annie took Mrs. Gladstone to her tent for a chat while Mr. Gladstone talked with Buffalo Bill, Nate Salsbury and a Sioux Indian chief, Red Shirt. Then, on May 6, three days before the show's regular opening, there was a command performance arranged for Queen Victoria's son, Edward, the Prince of Wales, who would later become King Edward VII, and a group of royalty and nobility. The guests included Edward's wife, the Princess Alexandra, and their children. When Annie Oakley was presented, Alexandra, instead of offering her hand to be kissed as was customary, took Annie's hand in her own and said, "What a wonderful little girl." When Annie met the prince, she bowed, and he also shook her hand warmly. At the command performance she enchanted the party, blasting every target with unerring aim.

When the show opened the big top was filled to capacity. Crowds from the surrounding countryside came on special trains. Then, on May 12, there was another command performance, this one for Queen Victoria herself. She and her party came in carriages from Windsor Castle. It was a glittering assemblage of royalty, including the rulers of Denmark, Greece, Saxony and Belgium and their wives; the crown princes of Germany, Austria and Sweden; and many princesses and princes of various countries of Europe.

Victoria was an enthusiastic spectator at the show and was

especially impressed by Annie Oakley's performance. Afterward, when Annie was presented, the queen said to her, "You are a very clever little girl." All this produced tremendous publicity, not only for the Wild West, but for Annie herself.

Among other royal and titled personages attending the regular shows was the Grand Duke Michael of Russia, who was then courting Princess Victoria, one of the daughters of Edward, Prince of Wales. Michael was an expert marksman and Edward arranged a trapshooting match for him with Annie. It was supposed to be kept secret, but Major Burke couldn't resist this opportunity for more publicity. He leaked the news of the shooting match to the newspapers.

Some of the newsmen saw it as something more than a test of shooting ability. It was well known that Edward did not favor a marriage between Grand Duke Michael and his daughter, and also that Britishers in general did not like the idea. These editors and reporters suspected that Edward hoped to see the grand duke humiliated as a result of losing to a woman.

Prince Edward, with a group of royalty and nobility, were spectators at the contest, held one morning at the showgrounds. Each contestant was to fire at fifty clay pigeons. Annie broke forty-seven of hers and Michael scored thirty-seven hits. A London newspaper printed the sly comment that Annie Oakley, with her "magic gun," was responsible for the grand duke's losing not one, but two matches—the shooting contest and the hand of the princess. And indeed, nothing further came of Michael's attempt to win Princess Victoria, whatever the true reason may have been.

The show stayed in London throughout the summer. Often, Annie would have a group of English mothers and their children to tea, also inviting some of the show's Indian children. She made a charming figure as she served her guests at tables set up on the grass in front of her tent.

All this publicity for Annie stirred Buffalo Bill's resentment again. Neither Annie nor Cody ever revealed what really happened, but when the Wild West moved from London to Birmingham at the end of October, Annie and Frank Butler were not on the train.

She and Frank spent a delightful fortnight as guests of R. Edward Clark, an English country gentleman, at his estate in Shrewsbury. Much refreshed, the Butlers returned to a London that seemed more cheery, intimate and friendly under the gray November skies than in the summer. After a few days there, they crossed the English Channel and journeyed to Paris. In the French capital they talked with a booking agent about a European engagement for them during the winter.

Meanwhile, Annie accepted an invitation to give a shooting demonstration before Emperor Wilhelm I of Germany. She and Frank traveled to Berlin. On a Sunday morning a courier escorted them to a carriage whose doors were emblazoned with the golden eagles of Germany's ruling house, the Hohenzollerns. They drove down the wide, impressive boulevard called the Unter den Linden, through the huge Brandenburg Gate and the wooded Tiergarten to the suburb of Charlottenburg on the River Spree, where the emperor's palace was located.

There, at the Charlottenburg Race Course, the gallery was filled with the Prussian officers who made the German army a powerful and much-feared military force. They sat stiffly in their gray uniforms and spiked helmets, not at all impressed by this little American girl who had the audacity to try to show them anything about marksmanship.

There was a message for Annie, expressing the emperor's regret that he was indisposed and could not attend. Annie then went ahead with her demonstration. The Prussians were silent as her act began. But they edged forward in their seats as she first broke every one of a series of clay pigeons sent whirling into the air; then a whole flock of live pigeons were released, soaring up in all directions. She shot every one of them. Finally, when Frank tossed up six glass balls and she smashed them all in midair, the stern-faced Prussians broke into loud applause.

All at once a man in a colonel's uniform stepped from the stands. Crown Prince Wilhelm of Germany made an impressive military figure in spite of his withered left arm that hung useless at his side, a defect suffered when he was born. An aide came up to Annie. In heavily accented, guttural English he told her what the prince commanded: She was to fire a bullet and put out a lighted cigarette held between his lips.

Crown Prince Wilhelm stood at a distance with the lighted cigarette in his mouth. There was complete silence in the gallery as Annie calmly raised her rifle and fired. The glowing tip of the cigarette was extinguished.

Newspapers throughout the world trumpeted the story in headlines. Nearly thirty years later, during World War I, Kaiser (Emperor) Wilhelm II, the crown prince of Annie's visit to Charlottenburg, was much hated for his role in the war. An American newspaperman dredged up the story of Annie Oakley and Crown Prince Wilhelm and wrote an article about it, suggesting that perhaps Annie would have done better to miss the cigarette tip but not Prince Wilhelm himself that day at Charlottenburg!

Annie hadn't realized it before, but the summer in London, for all its triumphs and good times, had tired her. In Berlin that night after the Charlottenburg visit, she was ill. An American doctor who was in Berlin examined her and shook his head when he took her pulse, temperature and blood pressure. She was suffering from exhaustion, he said, and must have complete rest.

Annie's next engagement, scheduled for Paris, was canceled. Within a day or so the Butlers were aboard a steamer, bound for New York.

That December of 1887, after their return to New York, the Butlers found accommodations at a small hotel near Madison Square. There, for the next two months, Annie had the rest she needed.

In February, Frank began to make the rounds of theatrical booking agents' offices in search of an engagement for Annie. He soon learned how quickly fame can fade. The agents he visited hardly seemed to remember Annie Oakley. Comparatively little had been heard of her while the Wild West was in Europe, and nothing at all during the two months of rest in New York.

Frank had to rely on shooting matches to bring Annie some much-needed publicity. It wasn't the kind of work Annie was used to, but the Butlers needed to make some money. One match, in Trenton, New Jersey, against a local champion, would pay the winner two hundred dollars in prize money. She and Frank went to Trenton, where she won before an unfriendly audience that cheered the Trenton expert and booed her.

However, New York newspapers reported her victory, and this was enough to get her a booking at one of New York's most popular theaters, Tony Pastor's Opera House on Fourteenth Street. Annie's act was the featured one on the playbill. It was like being back in vaudeville again, and the good salary and generous applause from large audiences helped lift Annie's spirits.

In the spring of 1888 Frank secured a contract for Annie as the featured star with Buckskin Joe's Wild West, a rival of Buffalo Bill. The show was barely making expenses when its roar tour reached Pittsburgh. There, still another wild West show, Pawnee Bill's, owned by Gordon W. Lillie, was stranded, deeply in debt. Frank Butler suggested that the two shows merge, and when the owners agreed the combined shows took to the road again under Pawnee Bill's name.

Annie kept the improved Pawnee Bill's Wild West alive almost single-handedly. She led the parades and the processions that opened the performance under the big top. Her act drew the loudest applause as she used every shooting trick she knew. She was the publicity agent, giving interviews to reporters. Under her leadership the show continued to the end of the summer.

In October the Butlers came back to New York City and a second engagement starring Annie at Tony Pastor's. When that ended there were more shooting matches. Then Annie obtained a leading part in a stage show, a western melodrama called *Deadwood Dick*.

The following spring, Annie received a letter from Nate Salsbury asking her to return to the Wild West. Buffalo Bill visited Annie in New York. The two settled their differences, and Annie signed a new contract with the Wild West. Cody took her in his arms, crying, "Little Missie!" Everybody with the show, down to the last roustabout, was happy that Annie was back.

A month later, in April 1889, the Wild West sailed on the liner *Persian Monarch* to Le Havre, France, and moved from there to Paris. "Gay Paree" was gayer than ever that summer.

France was celebrating the hundredth anniversary of the start of the French Revolution.

Along the Seine River, a tower of steel latticework soared gracefully nine hundred eighty-four feet into the air. The new Eiffel Tower was the tallest structure in Europe and a wonder of the world. Throughout the summer crowds stood in line to ride elevators to the top for the magnificent view or to dine in one of the restaurants located at several levels above the ground.

Another attraction was the International Exposition, with exhibits from many countries. The exposition grounds were near the Eiffel Tower, covering two hundred acres.

The Wild West occupied a thirty-acre space within sight of the exposition grounds. Not far away, in a wooded park, the Indians set up their tepees. Wealthy Parisians living in the exclusive residential district near the Arch of Triumph could watch the Wild West's steers, buffalo and horses in a corral close to the wide, splendid Avenue de la Grande Armée.

On opening day, May 18, a great crowd filled the seats in the arena. Annie Oakley, as usual, was a star attraction. At the conclusion of her act the audience stood up, shouting, *"Vive Annie Oakley!"*

Annie and the rest of the show fairly took Paris by storm. When midsummer came the seats were sold out long before show time each day. Paris department stores and shops profited handsomely by stocking Indian moccasins, blankets, bows and arrows, bearskins, buffalo robes, western saddles and lariats. Paris was in love with America's wild West.

In the fall, the Wild West left Paris and headed south. In Barcelona, Spain, near disaster struck. Epidemics of smallpox and influenza swept over the city. Audiences were small because people wouldn't risk appearing in public for fear of infection with one disease or the other. Half of the Wild West's people fell ill. When the Spanish authorities placed a quarantine on the city, no one was allowed to leave. The Wild West was trapped.

The Indian legend of death to those who crossed the ocean seemed to be coming true. Ten Indians died of flu. The others huddled in terror in their tepees, chanting the gloomy Indian death song. Then three roustabouts fell ill of smallpox and died. Annie Oakley was sick for a time but recovered.

At last, in January, Nate Salsbury prevailed upon the authorities to let the Wild West leave for Italy. The Italians gave the show a warm welcome and the Wild West performers enjoyed both the responsive audiences and the wonderful sightseeing available throughout the Italian tour. After Italy, the show moved to Switzerland, then Munich, Germany, and Vienna, Austria. In Vienna, for the first time in a European country, the audiences were small and displayed little enthusiasm for the show's attractions.

The second summer season in Europe began with performances in more than a dozen cities throughout Germany. Everywhere, the Germans appreciated Annie's skill with a gun.

On the whole, the Wild West's tour of Europe had been successful and profitable, and Nate Salsbury and Buffalo Bill decided to keep it abroad for another season.

This decision proved a mistake. The Indians were uneasy and wanted to go home. Word had reached them of the "Messiah craze" that was causing unrest among the western tribes. An Indian declaring himself the Indian Messiah said he had had a vision in which the buffalo of the Great Plains, almost wiped out as a result of senseless slaughter by white hunters, were restored to life when the Indians drove the white people from Indian lands. The Plains Indians held "ghost dances" and became greatly aroused against the whites. When law-enforcement officers tried to arrest Sitting Bull as a leader of the discontented Sioux, the chief resisted and was shot dead.

There was still more trouble brewing. An official in the Bureau of Indian Affairs in Washington brought completely false charges that Buffalo Bill was mistreating the show's Indians. American consular officials made visits of inspection to the winter quarters, and although they fond nothing wrong, the charges persisted in Washington. Finally, in disgust, Cody and Nate Salsbury sailed back to America and went to the capital, taking the Indians with them. They soon satisfied the Bureau of Indian Affairs officials that the charges were nonsense.

So the Wild West stayed on, wintering in Scotland before another European season. By now, the third winter of the tour, Annie was homesick. The raw Scottish weather and the big, drafty hall that was the show's headquarters did nothing to make her feel better. With the approach of the Christmas season she sought consolation in designing and preparing for a Glasgow printer a personal holiday card to send home to America. On one of its four pages, Annie had a verse of her own printed:

> I've built a bridge of the kindest thoughts
> Over the ocean so wide
> And all the good wishes keep rushing across
> From this to the other side.

On another page was a picture of herself with the caption: "Little Sure-Shot." The third page was titled "Christmas in the West," with a young girl waving to visitors arriving on a sled in a snow-covered landscape. The last page was headed: "Christmas in the East," and showed a scene of a wealthy man turning away hungry people from the door of his mansion. Annie still had not forgotten the poverty of her childhood.

In the fall, after another season abroad, the Wild West finally sailed for home.

THE SHOW GOES ON

Back in New York Annie and Frank decided that it was time to think about a home of their own.

They began watching the real-estate advertisements in the New York newspapers.

One advertisement offered land for sale in Nutley, New Jersey. Nutley was far enough from New York to be rustic, yet near enough so that the Butlers could easily go into the city. Annie and Frank were enchanted with Nutley. It was an old town, settled in the seventeenth century. Many of the original inhabitants were Dutch and some of their quaint, red and brown sandstone houses still stood in streets shaded by the trees that had given Nutley its name—walnut, beech, chestnut, oak, hickory and hazel. A stream flowed through the heart of the village. Along its banks stood ivy-covered gristmills, cotton and woolen mills beside the placid waters of millponds. Just to the east, beyond where the Passaic River flowed, the Watchung Hills rose in gentle elevations. And the Butlers were assured of congenial neighbors. Ever since the Civil War a colony of artists and writers had lived in Nutley in a residential park called the Enclosure.

Annie and Frank bought land on a street corner with many shade trees and immediately set a builder to work on their house. The house was different from most. For years Annie had been used to living out of trunks on the road. She decided it would be simpler to keep their things—she loved clothes and had a large wardrobe—in the trunks, so that getting ready to rejoin the Wild West would be an easy task. So the Nutley house had no closets.

In the spring of 1893 the Butlers moved in. They were immediately swept into the social life of Nutley's artistic residents. Something was going on all the time—costume balls, dances, tea parties, archery contests.

In spite of all the social activity, Annie found time to give shooting exhibitions and to appear again in an act at Tony Pastor's in Manhattan. Frank Butler had a job as a gun and ammunition salesman.

Ambitious plans were already being carried out for the Wild West's summer of 1893. Chicago was to be the scene of the World's Columbian Exposition during that summer, celebrating the four hundredth anniversary of Christopher Columbus's discovery of the New World. Salsbury asked for a concession on the exposition grounds for the Wild West. The Chicago World's Fair refused. Salsbury then leased fifteen acres right across from the fair's entrance.

Major Burke began publicity for the bigger and better new show that would entertain visitors to Chicago. It would have a horseshoe-shaped arena seating eighteen thousand people, five hundred performers, a herd of buffalo shipped in from Montana and a Congress of Rough Riders of the World.

The show opened in April at the World's Fair, with afternoon and evening performances. The Congress of Rough Riders was truly spectacular. It reflected America's growing involvement in international affairs and the American public's somewhat waning interest in a show limited to acts about the old wild West. It included American cavalry riders; French chasseurs, wearing scarlet breeches and blue coats; British lancers and German uhlans, who were also equipped with lances; fierce-eyed Cossacks, expert riders from the steppes of Russia, wearing heavy leather boots and armed with sabers; gauchos from the pampas of Argentina, dressed in bright-colored serapes and wearing wide-brimmed sombreros; Arab Bedouins in their hooded white burnooses, mounted on the matchless steeds of Arabia; and of course the more familiar American cowboys.

Mayor Carter Harrison of Chicago asked the World's Fair authorities to give the city's poor children a free day's outing at the fair. When they refused, Major Burke seized the opportunity to obtain excellent publicity for the show. The needy children would see the Wild West free of charge, he announced. He arranged for them to have free rides to the grounds on the excursion trains operated by the Illinois Central Railroad. In the Wild West arena there would be free reserved seats for the youngsters and they would have plenty of free candy and ice cream. On "Waif's Day" fifteen thousand children came. And before the show started, Annie Oakley delighted them with a guided tour through the Indian village on the grounds.

The newspaper stories about the children's day at the Wild

West attracted even greater crowds to the show in the days that followed. When September came and the show and its people prepared to leave Chicago, six million people had seen Buffalo Bill, Annie Oakley and the rest of the attractions.

All was not well with America that fall, however. Early in 1893 there had been several failures of large American companies, heralding one of the "panic years" that occurred before the United States government, almost forty years later, placed controls on speculation in the stock market and insured savings accounts. By the time the Wild West left Chicago there had been more failures. Banks closed, and people lost all their savings; the many unemployed went hungry.

Back home in Nutley, Annie and Frank took part in a charity circus for the benefit of the poor. People in America were showing an increasing concern with improving the lives of underprivileged and needy people, and this time of financial troubles inspired many such charitable affairs.

By the new year, the economic panic was subsiding and Annie and Frank began to look forward to another successful season with Buffalo Bill's Wild West.

The Butlers were disappointed in their hopes for another prosperous year for the show. An epidemic of smallpox threatened the New York City area, and all the people of the Wild West had to be vaccinated. That caused stiff and sore arms which made it difficult for many of them, including Annie herself, to perform properly. It was midsummer before everyone was back to normal. But even then the effects of the panic lingered. People had less money to spend on amusements, and the crowds under the big top were smaller than ever before.

Steps were taken to bring attendance up again. Annie introduced some new features into her act. For part of it she used a bicycle. The popularity of bicycles, first used in Paris about the year 1816, had spread across the ocean. In that year of 1894 their use in the United States was widespread, and many people belonged to bicycle clubs formed to promote racing and touring.

In Annie's act she rode around the ring holding her rifle in both hands as she raised it to shatter glass-ball targets. Then she would dismount, leap to her pony's back and continue her performance. Sometimes she would miss a shot on purpose, then pout and with a shrug of her shoulders proceed to break every one of a series of targets catapulted up by the powerful springs of a trap. It always delighted her audiences, and again it shows how strong her confidence in herself was. Suppose she had missed again . . . . No audience would have believed that was intentional. But when hitting a target was of vital importance, Annie didn't miss.

Annie began to worry about getting old. From the first her popularity had depended not only on her skill with firearms but on her appearance. People loved to see such a small, delicate young girl put bullets through targets with so much poise and precision, and Annie knew it. When she spoke at an informal banquet given her by New York City newsmen she said, "I would like to knock a few years off my age, for to tell the truth I am nearly twenty-eight." Actually she was then thirty-four.

Meanwhile, Major Burke arranged a series of publicity campaigns, and frequently involved Annie in his press conferences. In September he, Buffalo Bill, Annie and five Indians went to West Orange, New Jersey, to meet one of the greatest of modern inventors, Thomas A. Edison, who had invented the electric light and the phonograph as well as improvements in a host of devices. In his experimental laboratory in West Orange, Mr. Edison was working on another extraordinary idea.

The visitors were taken into a darkened room, where a spotlight was turned on. A laboratory assistant then cranked a kinetograph, the earliest type of motion-picture camera, and Annie did a pantomime of a shooting exhibition. Buffalo Bill and Indian Chief Short Bull talked in sign language. An Indian named Lost Horse went through the Buffalo Dance with much stamping of his feet. His companions shuffled before the camera in a war dance. These pantomimes were well suited to movie making, since at that time and for many years after motion pictures were silent.

Some weeks later the picture was shown to audiences in a darkened room on Broadway in New York. It was a forerunner of a type of motion picture that has been a favorite ever since—the Western.

In spite of these efforts, attendance flagged, and the Wild West ended its disappointing season in Brooklyn early in October. Nate Salsbury resigned as the show's business manager and his place was taken by a long-experienced showman, James A. Bailey, whose own circus had then become part of the big Barnum & Bailey Circus. He knew that the public's taste in tent shows was changing with the times; strictly "wild West" programs were no longer as popular as they had been. So Bailey added a feature to the big-top acts that was already used by regular circuses and had proved quite profitable—the side show, with its dwarfs, giants and other attractions. Bailey also knew the power of publicity to increase attendance, and hired an assistant to help Major Burke.

For the 1895 season the Wild West show once again opened at Madison Square Garden. Then came a long tour through New England, Pennsylvania, Kentucky, Virginia and seven Midwestern states.

In 1896 the show played throughout the summer at what was then the largest indoor stadium in the world, the new Coliseum in Chicago. That September it moved westward. In October "the little girl of the western plains" saw those plains for the first time in her life. The Wild West crossed the Missouri River to North Platte, Nebraska, the place where Buffalo Bill had started.

Thousands of people came in special trains to see the show and pay tribute to the man who had made the Far West live for the people of the East and Middle West.

That the show could perform profitably in the Far West was not due entirely to Cody's fame. The world of the old West had changed greatly by that year of 1896. Gone were the notorious badmen and outlaws of the years when the country of the Great Plains and the Rocky Mountains was being developed. Gone too were the famous scouts and Indian fighters like Kit Carson; only Cody himself was left. And many of the western towns that had been too small in earlier years to make tent show performances profitable were now good-sized cities where large audiences would attend.

Vast herds of cattle still grazed on the plains; but ranch owners now were primarily businessmen, and cowboys weren't the romantic figures they had been in earlier years. People in states west of the Mississippi River were now as amused as the easterners had once been by the shrill war whoops of the Wild West's Indians mounted on their ponies, swooping down on a bullet-scarred Deadwood mail coach in the circus arena; by the wrenching and twisting of riders trying to stay on the backs of bucking broncos; and by all the other reminders of the great days of the Far West's earlier years.

At Scout's Rest Ranch, the home Cody had built three miles north of North Platte, there were many reminders of those bygone days. Before the Wild West left, Cody took a group of the performers to the ranch for a festive day of celebrating.

Two years later, in the summer of 1898, the Wild West returned to Nebraska. In Omaha, "Cody Day" was celebrated, and Buffalo Bill was honored at numerous homecoming festivities.

Early in 1898 when the Spanish-American War began, Cody announced that he expected to rejoin the United States Army. He never did, but during the 1899 season he and Salsbury took advantage of the war and people's excitement over America's victory. When the show opened at Madison Square Garden, five hundred men reenacted the battle of San Juan Hill in Cuba that had turned the tide against the Spanish.

Then in 1900 Annie, too, enjoined a homecoming performance. The show's tour included a stop in Greenville, Ohio. The Wild West unloaded and set up for its performance in Armstrong's pasture. The next morning her mother and several of Annie's sisters who lived in western Ohio drove in and had lunch in her tent. They were so absorbed in their reunion that Annie missed the morning parade.

That afternoon twenty thousand people jammed into the big top to see Greenville's pride, Annie Oakley. She didn't disappoint them. They cheered her performance from beginning to end. Afterward, she was presented with a silver cup, engraved, "To Miss Annie Oakley, From Old Home Friends of Greenville, Ohio, July 25, 1900." Annie would never forget that day.

TRAGEDY

As the twentieth century began, Annie Oakley had been in show business nearly twenty-five years, over fifteen of them with the Wild West. Buffalo Bill was fifty-five years old, his hair almost snow-white, and some of his drive and energy had faded. Frank Butler, at fifty, was still an active man with a great zest for life, but he was slowing down. And Annie, while she could still make her audiences believe she was far younger than forty, had deep lines around her eyes, put there by years of squinting at targets in bright sunlight, and her hearing was damaged by constant explosions of gunfire.

Rehearsals for the 1901 season were held at the show's winter quarters in Bridgeport, Connecticut. More new spectacles had been added that year. Although none of them had much to do with the Far West, this was not due to any dimming of the West's glamour. Westerns, whether in books, stage plays or circuses like Buffalo Bill's, were still among the most popular of entertainments. The new features reflected increased public interest in star performers and acts from outside the country, now that the United States had become a major world power and people had a new curiosity about lands overseas.

The twentieth-century version of the show had a successful tour. By October 28 it had reached Charlotte, North Carolina. There was to be just one more stand for the Wild West that season, in Danville, Virginia. It was midnight when Annie and Frank rode in a carriage through the dark streets of Charlotte to the railroad station. They passed several of the heavy, slow-moving show wagons also bound there. Loading was nearly finished when they arrived and boarded their sleeping car, midway back from the locomotive of the second section. There was an occasional sound of hushed voices as those who were already aboard prepared for sleep. The porter had turned down the beds in the Butlers' stateroom, and a plate of sandwiches stood on a night table there. The warmth of the Pullman car was welcome after the ride through the chilly fall night.

Soon the first section pulled out of the station. When the second train moved out, Annie and Frank had gone to bed. Probably they were asleep when the engineer in the locomotive's cab eased his throttle gently ahead and the long train moved northward on the single main-line track. If they were still awake, the muffled clickety-click of the wheels on the rails would have been like a lullaby.

Ahead, the first section had passed through Lexington and Greensboro. The conductor of freight train Number 75, running south from Greensboro, somehow did not get a telegraphed order to wait on a siding until the other two show train sections had passed. His engineer pulled the long string of boxcars onto the main line and opened his throttle for the run to Charlotte.

Two and a half hours out of Charlotte, the second section was approaching Lexington. Suddenly, as it rounded a curve, the show train's engineer froze in terror and slammed on his air brakes—too late. For a brief instant the yellow eye of the freight locomotive's headlight glared at him. Then came the shock of the crash.

In the stateroom, Frank Butler was shaken roughly awake. He sat bolt upright in pitch darkness. Then, from outside, came the voices of men cursing. Frank shouted Annie's name. At first there was no response. Then, leaping out of bed, he realized that the stateroom had been shattered into twisted wreckage. His groping hand struck something, and he breathed a thankful prayer as Annie spoke: "I'm all right, Jimmy."

She was not all right. After wrapping a robe about her, Frank had to carry her into the sleeping car's passageway, which fortunately was still clear, and then outside. There they heard the screams of injured horses and the sound of gunshots as the animals were put out of their misery. Frank stared in horror at Buffalo Bill, a frantic figure in a purple dressing gown, his white locks streaming down to his shoulders in wild disorder. Cody stood looking at Old Pap, his beloved horse, twitching in torment. He spoke to a man nearby, took the rifle that was handed to him, and fired.

Miraculously, no one was killed, although four of the train's crew were injured. A great pit was dug in a cornfield alongside the track and Old Pap, the star ring horses and the rest of the dead animals were buried together in one grave. Only two of the horses in the second section lived to go into winter quarters in Bridgeport.

Annie was alive, but the collision had paralyzed her left side. And the events of that night caused her hair to turn white.

As soon as she could be moved, she was transferred to a hospital in Newark, New Jersey, where Frank could come every day from Nutley. There she underwent several operations. She left the hospital with a brace on her left leg. It was the end of Annie's career with Buffalo Bill and the Wild West.

Gradually, Annie learned to walk again. By the next spring she was able to get rid of her cane, and in the fall she paid a visit to the Nutley Gun Club.

She went inside and picked up a gun, cradling it lovingly. She started to return it to the rack, then hesitated and swung her weight forward on the braced leg, still holding the shotgun. She moved on to the club's target range. Annie asked the attendant to release a clay pigeon. As it sailed up, she raised the gun to her shoulder and fired. "Dead!" cried the attendant.

Annie was on the road back.

Although still not well enough to return to circus life, Annie was determined to get back into show business somehow. Frank Butler found the perfect solution: Annie would star in a melodrama, *The Western Girl*. This sort of stage performance would be less taxing than her old sharpshooting act, but it would still give her the chance to prove to audiences that she hadn't lost her skill with a gun and a lariat. The show opened on November 12, 1902, in Atlantic City, New Jersey. With her white hair dyed to its original chestnut color and her slim body dressed in a girlish fringed costume, Annie seemed young again in spite of the slight fault in her step. She held the audience rapt until the final curtain fell to a storm of applause. *The Western Girl* was not a great play, but Annie made it a success, and it stayed on the road for over a year.

Shortly after the play opened in 1902, the Butlers received sad news. Nate Salsbury had died in his New Jersey home on Christmas Eve of that year. The following spring brought more bad news for the Butlers. A Chicago newspaper had carried a shocking story that accused Annie of stealing a man's trousers and selling them to buy morphine. The story was promptly picked up and published by newspapers all over the United States. It was, of course, completely false. Someone on the Chicago newspaper's staff had jumped to conclusions when a woman named Elizabeth Cody was arrested for the crime. He concluded that Elizabeth Cody was really Buffalo Bill Cody's daughter-in-law and that she was really Annie Oakley. Annie and Frank filed suits against more than fifty newspapers that had printed the story. These suits dragged out for several years in the courts, but eventually Annie was awarded a total of over eight hundred thousand dollars for damages to her reputation.

By 1912 Annie was ready to go on the road with her old sharpshooting act, but it would not be with Buffalo Bill. Interest in Wild West shows had declined. In 1908 Cody had been forced to merge with Pawnee Bill's Historical Wild West. Cody was an old man by then, and in 1910, at the age of sixty-four, he retired. Without him and his appeal as the last of the Old West's scouts, the combined Wild West show went bankrupt and was taken over as part of Sells–Floto, a regular circus.

Annie and Frank accepted an offer from a new tent show

called Young Buffalo Wild West. They sold their house in Nutley and joined the show in Peoria, Illinois. It toured middle-western towns, Canada and the Atlantic seaboard. When it reached Cambridge, on the eastern shore of Maryland, Frank and Annie decided they had had enough of circus life. When the show's season ended, the Butlers bought a house near Cambridge.

They lived happily there for over two years. They bought a hunting dog, a setter they named Dave, and spent many days tramping the fields and tidal shores, hunting for game. During the long winter evenings they relaxed contentedly by the fire. It was a peaceful, idyllic life but eventually they had to go back to work to earn a living. In 1915 they decided to join the staff of the Carolina Hotel in Pinehurst, North Carolina.

Pinehurst had been a playground for wealthy people since 1895. The small village contained four hotels and numerous sport and recreation facilities that attracted visitors from the north during the winter months. There were four golf courses, tennis courts, large stables of the finest saddle and carriage horses as well as mounts for hunters, kennels of the best breeds of hunting dogs and plenty of game available in the beautiful countryside surrounding the village. Special express trains with luxurious Pullman cars made daily runs to Pinehurst from New York City and other points in the country.

Pinehurst proved a fine opportunity for the Butlers. Frank took charge of the trapshooting range and Annie gave target-shooting instructions to hotel guests. They also gave exhibitions, and their dog Dave had a leading part in these. At a signal he would trot up alongside Frank, who would place an apple on his head. Annie would then shoot the apple off with a bullet. Another of Annie's stunts was to dent brass discs that

Frank tossed into the air. Annie may have missed the fame and glory of her years as the world's greatest sharpshooter, but she was happy at Pinehurst and enjoyed sharing her special skill with others.

During each season there was a constant round of all sorts of activities—golf and tennis tournaments, horse races, shooting matches, dances, amateur theatrical productions and gymnastic exhibitions. Annie made use of her acting experience in the plays that were put on in the large, luxurious clubhouse, as well as in a minstrel show held each season.

Those who spent vacations at Pinehurst included noted figures in the world of arts, business and finance. While Annie and Frank were there they met such notables as John Philip Sousa, the bandleader and composer of military marches; Booth Tarkington, already famous as a writer, who would turn out over fifty successful novels and plays in his lifetime; and Edgar A. Guest, whose homely verses—of the same type that Frank Butler loved to write—were then appearing in his daily newspaper column. Most famous of all was a little old man who played golf every day—one of the richest men in the world—John D. Rockefeller, founder of the immense Standard Oil Company.

It was at Pinehurst, in January 1917, that Annie learned of the death of her friend and mentor, Buffalo Bill, the man who had shaped her life for more than a quarter of a century and who was, more than anyone else, responsible for her worldwide fame. To Annie, Buffalo Bill's death seemed the end of an era. In her tender farewell she wrote, "Goodbye, old friend. The setting sun beyond the western hills will pay daily tribute to the last great pioneer of the West."

10

THE END
OF THE TRAIL

In the autumn of 1922 Annie was 62 years old. She was not well. Her doctor suggested a warmer climate, so Annie and Frank sailed south in a steamer to Jacksonville, Florida, en route to Leesburg. With them went their old dog, Dave, and also a young hunting dog they had recently bought.

Leesburg is in the rolling countryside of west-central Florida. The town is set between two of the many lakes that interlace that region. The pine forests and open country in its surrounding area make it a hunter's paradise. Annie and Frank were looking forward to it.

Friends of the Butlers from Leesburg met them on the pier in Jacksonville. On the drive to Leesburg the car struck a soft shoulder at the edge of the road and turned over. Only Annie was seriously injured. She was rushed to a hospital, where she lay for weeks with a dislocated hip and fractured ankle. After several more weeks in a wheelchair, she was finally able to hitch herself about on crutches, but once again she had to wear a leg brace. There would be no more hunting for Annie.

Frank Butler did go into the woods now and then during Annie's convalescence. His heart wasn't in these lonely rambles, but he continued to hunt because Annie seemed to enjoy hearing about his adventures.

One day in February Frank took off for the woods with the young hunting dog at his heels. Old Dave, suffering with a lame shoulder, remained at Annie's feet on the hotel porch. Frank was later than usual returning that day and Dave became uneasy. He rose, trotted off the porch and went down the road Frank had taken when he left. As he started across an intersection, a car came out of the side road. There was a loud screech of brakes.

In his years with Annie and Frank, Dave had become like a member of the family. Their eyes were filled with unashamed tears as they buried their old friend under the pines in back of the hotel.

Annie and Frank stayed in Leesburg three years. Annie's thoughts kept turning to her girlhood in Darke County. Finally, in April of 1926, she and Frank boarded a train for Ohio. There would be no returning to the old farm, for Annie's mother and stepfather were dead and the farm had been sold. But Annie's half sister, Emily Patterson, lived in Dayton, not too many miles away. She welcomed the Butlers warmly.

The journey from Florida had so exhausted Annie that she was completely bedridden. Now, more than ever, Frank was her anchor.

One day he brought a visitor. In walked a lanky, long-legged figure with a shock of unruly hair and a smile that had captivated thousands—Will Rogers. Annie and the famous entertainer and newspaper columnist had become fast friends during a summer visit by the Butlers to Long Island.

A few days later Frank brought a newspaper clipping—one of Will Rogers's columns. It was about Annie. Rogers gave her address in Dayton and told his readers to write to her, now confined with a new ailment. Frank put the clipping into the trunk where Annie kept others, as well as programs, photographs and fan letters. Annie decided that she ought to sort out all her memorabilia and Frank engaged a college girl to help with the job.

It was about this time that Annie learned she was suffering from pernicious anemia, a disease for which there was no cure. She felt that she wanted to be nearer her childhood home in Darke County, and was delighted when her niece, Bonnie Blakeley, offered to have Annie at her home in the village of Ansonia, eight miles north of Greenville. During the summer of 1926 as Annie lay in bed there, she wrote many letters to the friends she had made throughout her career.

Frank stayed at a hotel in Greenville. His health was not good, either, but he came to see Annie as often as he could.

Annie grew weaker as the summer wore on. At the end of August she needed a full-time nurse. Since her niece's house didn't have accommodations where a nurse could be close to her bed, Annie was forced to move again. Two teachers, old family friends, owned a roomy frame house in Greenville. They were willing to have Annie stay with them and Annie was glad to accept their offer. It would be easier for Frank to visit her there.

Annie knew that she wasn't going to live very long. She didn't want to discuss it with Frank, who never liked to think about death. So she herself made arrangements to buy two burial plots in a little country cemetery.

Those last days were a time of mixed emotions for Annie. She had been drawn back to Ohio by memories that were dear to her—of her family, the little cabin that had been her childhood home, the woods and meadows where she had hunted the grouse and quail that had started her on the road to success. Yet part of Annie Oakley had not come home but had stayed with Buffalo Bill's Wild West in the days when she had been "the little girl of the western plains," known to millions as "Little Sure-Shot." That part of her life was recaptured as she pored over the great store of newspaper clippings about her career that she had accumulated over the years. For much of the time, in Annie's thoughts as she lay in bed, she was once again on the road with the show that had been her life for so long.

With Frank helping her, Annie tied her clippings in bundles. She wanted one of her oldest and best friends, the noted actor Fred Stone, to take charge of them, and they were sent to him in New York. Then Annie wrote some instructions for Frank concerning her will and some bonds and securities that would go to him when she died.

It was near the end of October, a rainy afternoon when the wind had a sharp edge, that Annie heard Frank's faltering steps, even slower than usual, on the stairs to her room. When he came in she saw the weariness on his face and realized what she must do. She told Frank he should go back to Florida, where the warm sun would help restore his health. Frank was unwilling to leave her at first, but finally he agreed.

The next day he took a train to New Jersey. At a bank in Newark he carried out Annie's instructions for her will and securities. He still felt reluctant to go off to Florida without Annie and he dreaded having to make the trip alone. Finally, he decided to call Annie's niece, Fern Campbell, who had lived with the Butlers in Nutley for several years. Fern was now living in Detroit. She immediately invited Frank to stay with her until she could arrange to take him south herself.

Frank Butler never made it to Florida. He was still in Detroit on November 3, when word came from Greenville that Annie had died peacefully in her sleep. Frank died just a few weeks later, on November 23.

Annie's body was cremated after a funeral service in Greenville. Frank's body was sent there from Detroit, and they were buried together in the little cemetery in Brock, Ohio.

Will Rogers wrote a moving tribute to Annie for his newspaper column:

She was the acknowledged headliner for years in the great Buffalo Bill Show, the best known woman in the world at one time, for when she was with the show it toured everywhere. She was not only the greatest rifle shot for a woman that ever lived, but I doubt if her character could be matched anywhere outside of a saint. . . .

I had heard cowboys who had traveled with the Bill Show speak of her almost in reverence. They loved her. She was a marvelous woman, kindest hearted, most thoughtful, a wonderful Christian woman.

I went out to see her last Spring in Dayton. She was in bed, had been for months; but she was just as cheerful. I told her I would see her this Fall when I came back, and tried to cheer her in the usual dumb way I have of doing such things. She said I wouldn't, but "I'll meet you." Well, she will certainly keep her end of the bargain.

The End of the Trail

Annie Oakley's death did not mean that she was forgotten. Within a year after her death the first of several books about her was published, and over the years Annie has been portrayed on the stage, in movies and television and even in comic books.

A great many changes had taken place in America during the sixty-six years of Annie Oakley's life. When Annie was born in 1860, westward expansion was in progress. The pioneers who made their way to the Far West represented the true spirit of enterprise that made America great. They met and conquered a host of difficulties and dangers and often enough for these rugged settlers, life was a matter of pure survival.

Once they were established, their little settlements grew into towns and cities. Through hard work, intelligence and ingenuity they were able to take advantage of the many opportunities the young, ambitious nation offered. They adapted themselves to the changing conditions and grew along with the country which, by the beginning of the twentieth century, was a major world power.

This was the world of Annie Oakley. From her early years of poverty to the vaudeville stage, from star billing (and world renown) in the Wild West show to her teaching career, Annie's life both reflected and was a reflection of the changing American scene. As the nation developed and prospered, so did Annie. Her story, like the country's, was one of struggle and triumph; her spirit of energy, ambition and optimism that of America's golden era.

BIBLIOGRAPHY

ADAMS, RAMON F. *The Old-Time Cowhand*. New York: Macmillan, 1961.

ATHERTON, LEWIS. *The Cattle Kings*. Bloomington, Ind.: Indiana University Press, 1961.

BILLINGTON, RAY ALLEN. *The Far Western Frontier, 1830–1860*. New York: Harper & Row, 1956.

CODY, WILLIAM FREDERICK. *An Autobiography of Buffalo Bill*. New York: Holt, Rinehart & Winston, 1920 (reissued, 1969).

COOPER, COURTNEY RYLEY. *Annie Oakley, Woman at Arms*. New York: Duffield & Co., 1927.

CURTI, MERLE; SHRYOCK, RICHARD H.; COCHRAN, THOMAS C.; HARRINGTON, FRED HARVEY. *An American History*. New York: Harper & Row, 1950.

DAY, DONALD. *Will Rogers: A Biography*. New York: David McKay, 1962.

——— (Editor). *The Autobiography of Will Rogers*. Chicago: People's Book Club, 1949.

Bibliography

FLORY, CLAUDE R. "Annie Oakley in the South." *The North Carolina Historical Review*, Vol. XLIII, No. 3 (Summer, 1966).

GARST, SHANNON. *Buffalo Bill*. New York: Messner, 1948.

HAVIGHURST, WALTER. *Annie Oakley of the Wild West*. New York: Macmillan, 1954.

——— *The Heartland: Ohio, Indiana, Illinois*. New York: Harper & Row, 1969.

JOSEPHY, ALVIN M., JR. *The Indian Heritage of America*. New York: Knopf, 1971.

LYON, PETER. *The Wild, Wild West*. New York: Funk & Wagnalls, 1969.

PARKMAN, FRANCIS. *The Oregon Trail: Sketches of Prairie and Rocky Mountain Life*. Boston: Little, Brown, 1910.

ROOSEVELT, THEODORE. *The Winning of the West*. New York: Hastings House, 1963.

RUSSELL, DON. *The Lives and Legends of Buffalo Bill*. Norman: University of Oklahoma Press, 1960.

SAYERS, ISABELLE. *The Rifle Queen*. Ostrander, Ohio: Privately printed, 1973.

SEIDMAN, LAWRENCE IVAN. *Once in the Saddle*. New York: Knopf, 1973.

SELL, HENRY BLACKMAN and WEYBRIGHT, VICTOR. *Buffalo Bill and the Wild West*. New York: Oxford University Press, 1955.

SWARTWOUT, ANNIE FERN. *Missie: The Life and Times of Annie Oakley*. Blanchester, Ohio: Brown Publishing Co., 1947.

WESTERMEIER, CLIFFORD P. (Editor). *Trailing the Cowboy*. Caldwell, Idaho: Caxton Printers, Ltd., 1955.

(No author) *The Municipalities of Essex County, New Jersey*. New York: Lewis Historical Publishing Co., 1925.

(No author) Miscellaneous news stories. *The Pinehurst Outlook*, Vol. XVIII, No. 1 (Early Season Number), 1914-5.

INDEX

Index

Index

Index

CLIFFORD LINDSEY ALDERMAN was born and grew up in Springfield, Massachusetts. A graduate of the United States Naval Academy at Annapolis, Maryland, he served as a commander in World War II. He is the author of many books for young people on aspects of American history, including *The Dark Eagle: The Story of Benedict Arnold; Rum, Slaves and Molasses: The Story of New England's Triangular Trade; Colonists for Sale: The Story of Indentured Servants in America; The Rhode Island Colony* and *The Royal Opposition*. A long-time resident of New York, Mr. Alderman now lives in Pinellas Park, Florida.